SMOKING

Quarto.com

© 2025 Quarto Publishing Group USA Inc.
Text © 1996 Cheryl Alters Jamison and Bill Jamison,
© 2004 Paul Kirk and Bob Lyon, © 2009 Ardie A. Davis

First Published in 2025 by The Harvard Common Press,
an imprint of The Quarto Group,
100 Cummings Center, Suite 265-D,
Beverly, MA 01915, USA.
T (978) 282-9590 F (978) 283-2742

The Harvard Common Press titles are also available at
discount for retail, wholesale, promotional, and bulk
purchase. For details, contact the Special Sales Manager
by email at specialsales@quarto.com or by mail at
The Quarto Group, Attn: Special Sales Manager, 100
Cummings Center, Suite 265-D, Beverly, MA 01915, USA.

29 28 27 26 25   1 2 3 4 5

ISBN: 978-0-7603-9745-9

Digital edition published in 2025
eISBN: 978-0-7603-9746-6

Library of Congress Cataloging-in-Publication Data

Names: Harvard Common Press, editor.
Title: Smoking / editors of the Harvard Common Press.
Description: Beverly, MA, USA : Harvard Common Press,
2025. | Series: Great
  cooking outdoors | Cover title. | Includes
bibliographical references
  and index.
Identifiers: LCCN 2024054044 | ISBN 9780760397459
(hardcover)
Subjects: LCSH: Smoking (Cooking) | Outdoor cooking.
| Barbecuing.
Classification: LCC TX609 .S566 2025 | DDC
641.6/165--dc23/eng/20241205
LC record available at https://lccn.loc.gov/2024054044

The content in this book was previously published in
Sublime Smoke by Cheryl and Bill Jamison (Harvard
Common Press, 2004), *Paul Kirk's Championship
Barbecue* by Paul Kirk (Harvard Common Press, 2004),
and *25 Essentials: Techniques for Smoking* by
Ardie Davis (Harvard Common Press, 2017).

Design and Page Layout: Megan Jones Design
Photography: Michael Piazza on pages 26, 31, 37, 44, 56,
    59, 60, 63, 64, 80, 83, 90, 93, 101, 102, 112, 115, 117, 119,
    120, and 123; and Shutterstock on pages 12, 15, 16,
    19, 20, 23, 24, 29, 32, 35, 39, 40, 43, 47, 48, 51, 52, 55,
    67, 68, 72, 75, 77, 78, 84, 87, 89, 94, 97, 98, 105, 106,
    109, and 110
Illustration: Michael Korfhage

Printed in China

SMOKING

EDITORS OF THE HARVARD COMMON PRESS

HARVARD
COMMON
PRESS

CONTENTS

1

BARBECUE SAUCES

13

2

BBQ PORK FROM CLASSIC TO NEW

27

3

SMOKY BEEF AND LAMB

57

4
CHICKEN, TURKEY, AND OTHER BIRDS
81

5
FISH IN THE SMOKER
99

6
VEGETABLES AND BEANS IN THE SMOKER
113

INTRODUCTION: SMOKING BASICS

Drop the word *barbecue* into any gathering and you'll stir up a hubbub of chatter about who makes it best. Most people think theirs is the best, or that the best is sold at a little rib joint they have frequented in their hometown since childhood.

There's a lot of hype in the world of barbecue. Boasts of "world famous," "legendary," "award winning," and "world champion" abound. Newcomers to barbecue could easily get the impression that the field is too crowded with famous, award-winning, world-champion legends to make room for more. Don't be discouraged by the hoopla. There is room around the pit for you. You'll find that barbecuers are among the friendliest people on earth. They love to share what they know with anyone who wants to learn.

HOW TO BARBECUE RIBS

Start the charcoal 30 minutes before you want to put your ribs on the pit, then begin the slather and rub process. After you've arranged the hot charcoal to one side for indirect cooking and added a couple of wood chunks, drop the top grill into place and place the rib rack with the rib slots slanting away from the charcoal so that the first slot has at least 1 inch (2.5 cm) of clearance from the charcoal. Now, gingerly place each slab in a slot with the meat side facing the heat. Yes, it's a messy business and the

ends with the shortest ribs will curl around a bit. Either wipe your hands with one of the paper towels or lick your fingers, if nobody's looking, before you put the lid of the kettle on. Otherwise, the handle will be a mess, as will everything else you touch. With the lid on, you should get the great smell of hardwood smoke passing across barbecuing meat for the next hour. If the smoke dies away, drop in two more wood chunks at the first "hot" fuel addition.

It takes a minimum of 4 hours for loin backs or baby backs and 5 for spareribs to be done, although an hour longer for each is more likely, depending on air temperature, wind, and altitude. Check the charcoal every 45 minutes to an hour if you're using chunk charcoal. If you need to ignite briquettes, start them 20 minutes before you need to add fuel.

When the rub has set, about halfway through the cooking time, begin to baste the ribs every 30 minutes or so with plain apple juice or a sauce. Apply the baste with a spray bottle, mop it on with a dish mop, or sop it on with a clean cloth dipped into the baste.

At the second addition of fuel, it's time to shift the positions of the ribs, moving the front slab to the third slot and that slab to the front. The second and fourth slabs could also change slots. If the meat on the bones at the top of the ribs has started to pull away, the slabs should be inverted, because the temperature at the top of the ribs is hotter than it is at grill level. If the meat hasn't started to pull away, this

change of position can wait until the third fuel addition. With all this shifting, be sure to keep the meat side facing the heat.

A medium-dark-brown color, bones exposed top and bottom, and enough cooking time all signal the doneness of the ribs. Pull the slab you think is the most done and put it on a clean cutting board. Cut the first two ribs from where you cut off the breastbone and taste the meat. If the meat doesn't yet pull away cleanly from those bones, the ribs aren't done and require another 30 minutes to an hour of cooking time, but with no increase in heat. Return the slab to its slot.

When you finally pull the ribs, let them rest (set) for at least 10 minutes. Rib meat will shred if you cut the ribs too soon after they've come off the pit. Cut them meat side down with a sharp boning knife; wipe it off with a paper towel and touch it up with a steel between slabs. Have room-temperature barbecue sauce on the side for those who need it, but don't destroy the taste of your handiwork by smothering it in sauce, as if you had something to hide.

How to Glaze Ribs

If you want to glaze your ribs with barbecue sauce, at the almost-done stage (30 minutes before they should be coming off the pit), pull one slab from its slot and put it on the cutting board, meat side down. Brush your favorite barbecue sauce over it lightly. Turn it over and repeat the process on the meat side. Return it to its slot in the rib rack (another messy procedure requiring finger wiping or licking). When the time comes to taste the ribs, you can decide, when your guests have tested samples both ways, whether you want to repeat the process in the future. Many cooks do it in competition only. Feel ambitious? Try different barbecue sauces on two slabs of ribs.

HOW TO BARBECUE PORK BUTT

Cooking pork butt can be done the same way as ribs, over an indirect fire with a temperature between 230°F (110°C) and 250°F (120°C) for 8 to 16 hours, depending on how big the butt is and whether it is bone-in or boneless. A boned pork butt slow smokes to tender doneness in about 1½ hours per pound. The timing for a bone-in pork butt is 2 hours per pound.

Turn and rotate the butt at 4 hours or half of the projected cooking time. When the rub has set, about halfway through cooking, begin to baste every 30 minutes or so with plain apple juice or a sauce. Apply the baste with a spray bottle, mop it on with a dish mop, or sop it on with a clean cloth dipped into the baste.

Turn and rotate the butt again at 6 hours, or 2 more hours, then again at 7 hours, then finish cooking. Baste with apple juice when you turn the meat the first time, then baste every hour or when you replenish your fire.

TYPES OF HARDWOODS AND THEIR FLAVORS

Barbecuers on the contest circuit often find that it's easier to smoke with the woods available in their area, especially if they're using sticks or logs. If you're using wood chunks, chips, or pellets, these are readily available at barbecue and grill shops, at hardware stores, and by mail order.

Alder: From the Pacific Northwest, alder has a light, aromatic flavor. Alder and salmon are a match made in heaven. Planks made from alder are used to cook salmon and other fish.

Apple and Cherry: From the temperate regions of the United States, apple and cherry produce smoke that is a little sweeter and fruitier, which makes them good to use with chicken, turkey, and pork. Sometimes you can get wood directly from an orchard when the fruit trees are being pruned.

Hickory: From Pennsylvania to Kansas, Minnesota to Arkansas, hickory is very popular in Southern-style barbecue and lends a strong, hearty wood smoke flavor to ribs, sausage, pork butt, brisket, and whole chickens.

Maple: From New England and the Midwest, maple smolders to a sweeter, milder smoke that pairs well with chicken, vegetables, and fish.

Mesquite: From the Southwest, mesquite burns fast and hot, with a heavy smoke flavor. Mesquite is better for grilling than for smoking because it's harder to control for long smoking times. Too much mesquite for too long and your food is inedible.

Oak: From the temperate regions of the United States, oak, next to hickory, is probably the second-most common wood used in barbecue because it gives a wonderful smoke aroma without being bitter. It also pairs well with other woods.

Pecan: From the South and Midwest, pecan smolders to a mellow, rich aroma, which professional chefs love to use in their restaurants. It's also not overly smoky.

SMOKING TIMETABLE

This chart will give you an idea of how long foods take to smoke at around 230°F to 250°F (110°C to 120°C). The better you can control your fire and thus the temperature, the more reliable these cooking times will be.

Pork ribs: Baby back	1½ lbs (680 g)	3 to 5 hours
Pork ribs: Baby back	1¾ to 2¼ lbs (794 g to 1 kg)	4 to 6 hours
Spareribs	2½ to 3-plus lbs (1.1 to 1.4-plus kg)	5 to 7 hours
Whole pork shoulder	12 to 16 lbs (5.4 to 7.3 kg)	24 to 32 hours
Pork (Boston) butt	6 to 8 lbs (2.7 to 3.5 kg)	8 to 12 hours
Pork loin	8 to 10 lbs (3.5 to 4.5 kg)	12 to 15 hours
Pork tenderloin	1½ to 2 lbs (680 to 900 g)	2½ to 3 hours
Whole hog	up to 85 lbs (39 kg)	16 to 18 hours
Whole hog	85 to 135 lbs (39 to 61 kg)	18 to 24 hours
Pork sausage	1½- to 2½-inch (3.75 to 5.25 cm) diameter	1 to 3 hours
Beef tenderloin	3 to 4 lbs (1.4 to 1.8 kg)	3½ to 4 hours
Beef brisket	8 to 12 lbs (3.5 to 5.4 kg) trimmed	12 to 18 hours
Lamb (leg)	7 to 9 lbs (3.2 to 4 kg)	4 to 8 hours
Cabrito	8 to 12 lbs (3.5 to 5.4 kg)	4 to 5 hours
Chicken (whole)	2½ to 3 lbs (1.1 to 1.4 kg)	3 to 4 hours
Chicken (whole)	3½ to 4½ lbs (1.6 to 1.8 kg)	3 to 5 hours
Chicken (breast)	5 to 8 oz (140 to 225 g)	1 to 3 hours
Turkey (whole)	10 to 12 lbs (4.5 to 5.4 kg)	7 to 8 hours
Duck (whole)	4 to 5 lbs (1.8 to 2.3 kg)	3½ to 4 hours
Fish (whole)	4 to 6 lbs (1.8 to 2.3 kg)	3½ to 4 hours
Fish (fillets)	4 to 6 oz (115 to 170 g)	1½ to 2 hours

DONENESS CHART FOR SMOKING

Knowing at what internal temperature your smoked food is done is crucial. You want succulent, moist, tender barbecue—not dried-out jerky. Some cuts, such as beef tenderloin and leg of lamb, can be smoked to rare, medium rare, or well done. Most other meats and fish are smoked to a well-done tenderness. For ribs, the doneness test is visual—when the rib meat has pulled back about an inch (2.5 cm) from the bone. Use heat-safe meat thermometers inserted into brisket or pork butt and left in during smoking as well as instant-read thermometers quickly inserted into foods and then removed to check internal temperatures. For whole chickens, duck, and turkey, insert an instant-read thermometer into both the breast and the thigh. For cabrito, whole lamb, and whole hog, insert a fork into the hindquarter and twist to check for tenderness. Fish is done when it begins to flake when tested with a fork in the thickest part.

Pork ribs, any type	Meat pulls back from bone
Pork shoulder	195°F to 205°F (90°C to 100°C) to pull; 165°F to 185°F (75°C to 85°C) to slice
Pork (Boston) butt	195°F to 205°F (90°C to 100°C) to pull; 165°F to 185°F (75°C to 85°C) to slice
Pork tenderloin	155°F to 160°F (65°C to 70°C)
Pork loin	155°F to 160°F (65°C to 70°C)
Whole hog	185°F (85°C)
Pork sausage	165°F (75°C)
Beef brisket	185°F to 195°F (85°C to 90°C)
Beef tenderloin	130°F to 140°F (55°C to 60°C) medium rare; 150°F (65°C) medium; 160°F (70°C) well-done
Lamb (leg)	135°F (55°C) rare; 140°F (60°C) medium rare; 150°F (65°C) medium; 160°F (70°C) well-done
Cabrito	170°F to 180°F (75°C to 80°C)
Chicken	165°F (75°C)
Turkey	165°F (75°C)
Duck	165°F (75°C)

1

BARBECUE SAUCES

BARE BONES BARBECUE SAUCE

MAKES: About 2 cups (470 ml)

This sauce recipe can be used by anyone as a base from which to develop their own signature barbecue sauce.

....

1. Combine all the ingredients in a medium-size nonreactive saucepan and blend well. Bring to boil, reduce the heat to medium-low, and simmer for 30 minutes to let the flavors blend, stirring occasionally.

2. Now add ¼ to ½ teaspoon of your favorite spice, maybe some chili powder; start experimenting to develop your own championship barbecue sauce.

1 cup (240 g) tomato ketchup

½ cup (115 g) firmly packed light brown sugar

3 tablespoons (45 ml) distilled white vinegar

2 tablespoons (30 ml) water

1 tablespoon (15 ml) Worcestershire sauce

1 teaspoon non-iodized salt

½ teaspoon garlic powder

¼ teaspoon onion powder

- ⅓ cup (68 g) bacon drippings (bacon grease)
- 1 medium-size onion, minced
- 1 cup (240 g) tomato ketchup
- ½ cup (120 ml) water
- ⅓ cup (80 ml) fresh lemon juice (3 to 4 lemons)
- ¼ cup (60 g) firmly packed light brown sugar
- 2 tablespoons (30 ml) Worcestershire sauce
- 1 tablespoon (7 g) sweet Hungarian paprika
- 1 teaspoon fine sea salt
- 1 teaspoon freshly ground black pepper

BARBECUE SAUCE FOR CHICKEN

MAKES: About 3⅓ cups (785 ml)

This sauce is a good one for the backyard chef to start with. Try it on grilled or smoked chicken wings.

....

Heat the bacon drippings in a medium-size nonreactive saucepan over medium heat, then add the onion and cook, stirring, until soft but not browned. Add the remaining ingredients and blend well. Bring to a boil, then reduce the heat to medium-low and simmer for 30 minutes to let the flavors blend.

CAROLINA VINEGAR BARBECUE SAUCE

MAKES: About 1 cup (235 ml)

This sauce, traditional in the Carolinas, is great served on the side with chopped or pulled barbecue pork.

....

Combine all the ingredients in a small nonreactive saucepan and bring to a boil. Reduce the heat to medium-low and simmer for 15 minutes.

1 cup (235 ml) cider vinegar

2 tablespoons (26 g) granulated cane sugar

1 tablespoon (6 g) dry mustard

1 teaspoon crushed red pepper

1 teaspoon fine sea salt

1 teaspoon freshly ground black pepper

½ teaspoon celery salt

2 cups (480 g) tomato ketchup

¼ cup (60 g) firmly packed dark brown sugar

¼ cup (60 ml) apple juice

¼ cup (60 ml) cider vinegar

Juice of 1 lemon

1 teaspoon grated lemon zest

½ teaspoon fine sea salt

½ teaspoon freshly ground black pepper

SWEET AND MILD BARBECUE SAUCE

MAKES: About 3 cups (705 ml)

This is a good beginning barbecue sauce to use on barbecued ribs and brisket or grilled hot dogs.

Combine all the ingredients in a medium-size nonreactive saucepan, bring to a boil, reduce the heat to medium-low, and simmer until heated through, 15 to 20 minutes.

SMOKY BARBECUE SAUCE

MAKES: About 4 cups (940 ml)

This is a good basting, finishing, and dipping sauce for barbecued pork ribs, pork loin, and pulled pork. Add the liquid smoke until the sauce is to your taste. If you live in the Pacific Northwest, you'll probably add ¼ cup (60 ml)!

....

In a medium-size nonreactive saucepan, combine all the ingredients and bring to a boil. Reduce the heat to medium-low and simmer, stirring occasionally, for 20 minutes.

2 cups (480 g) tomato ketchup

1 cup (235 ml) cider vinegar

1 stick (½ cup [112 g]) unsalted butter

¼ cup (60 ml) Worcestershire sauce

1 to 2 tablespoons (15 to 30 ml) liquid smoke flavoring, to your taste

2 teaspoons granulated onion

2 teaspoons Louisiana hot sauce

1 teaspoon fine sea salt

1 teaspoon freshly ground black pepper

½ teaspoon granulated garlic

¼ teaspoon cayenne pepper

3 cups (720 g) tomato ketchup

½ cup (115 g) firmly packed light brown sugar

½ cup (170 g) molasses

¼ cup (44 g) prepared yellow mustard

2 tablespoons (30 ml) fresh lemon juice

2 tablespoons (30 ml) Worcestershire sauce

2 tablespoons (30 ml) liquid smoke flavoring

2 teaspoons granulated onion

1 teaspoon granulated garlic

1 teaspoon fine sea salt

1 teaspoon freshly ground black pepper

½ teaspoon cayenne pepper

MEMPHIS-STYLE SMOKY BARBECUE SAUCE

MAKES: About 5 cups (1,175 ml)

This is a sauce with that Southern barbecue vinegar twang, straight from Beale Street with some rhythm and blues. In Memphis, you order your ribs "wet" or "dry." Wet means with sauce, dry means with just the dry rub and the sauce on the side. In addition to ribs, serve this sauce with pulled pork, pork loin, or chicken.

....

Combine all the ingredients in a large nonreactive saucepan over medium heat and simmer for 20 minutes, stirring occasionally.

2

BBQ PORK FROM CLASSIC TO NEW

BASIC BARBECUED RIBS

SERVES: 6 to 8

If you prefer to use another style of ribs than spareribs, that's fine. It is quite all right to substitute other rib styles in any of these recipes.

··

1. Prepare an indirect fire.

2. Prepare the ribs by removing the membrane and trimming them of large pieces of fat. Season on all sides with the salt and rub it in. Season with the pepper and rub it in. Don't forget to season under the skirt.

3. Place the ribs on the pit, cover, and cook according to the Introduction (page 6).

4. Half an hour before the end of cooking, glaze the bone side of the slabs lightly with the barbecue sauce, turn, glaze the meat side, and cook 10 to 15 minutes longer. Lightly glaze the meat side again, turn, and cook 10 to 15 minutes longer.

5. Remove from the grill and let rest for 10 minutes before cutting into individual ribs. These are best served hot but still taste dandy served cold.

3 slabs 3.8 and down pork spareribs

3 tablespoons (54 g) salt, or to taste

2 tablespoons (12 g) freshly ground black pepper, or to taste

3 cups (705 ml) barbecue sauce of your choice

CLASSIC BARBECUED SPARERIBS

SERVES: 8

Tough, meaty spareribs from the side of the hog are the cheapest and thus the best to slow smoke. You can slow smoke more naturally tender baby back ribs (from along the backbone), but there's something really satisfying about turning a tough ol' slab o' spareribs into something to brag about. Look for meaty ribs without any exposed bone—no "shiners." If your ribs are frozen, thaw them in the refrigerator.

This technique involves a three-step process: Trim, skin, and smoke. Some barbecuers like to marinate their ribs before smoking; others like to add a zesty rub. Try ribs this simple way first, then go chase your moonbeam. When you want to cook several slabs of ribs and your grill can't accommodate them horizontally, invest in a rib rack, which is like a toast rack, but for ribs. Ribs smoke just as well vertically as they do horizontally. You can also stack them, one on top of the other; if you stack, change the position of the ribs every 45 minutes. Because the ribs need to smoke for a minimum of 3 hours, this recipe is not for a gas grill.

....

2 full slabs pork spareribs

½ cup (67 g) freshly ground black pepper

2 tablespoons (29 g) fine sea salt

1 teaspoon granulated garlic

½ cup (120 ml) canola oil

1 cup (90 g) wood chips, soaked in water and drained

Barbecue sauce of your choice for serving

1. To trim the spareribs, place them bone side up on a cutting board. Using a sharp butcher knife, slice off the flap of meat and save it. Next, if there's a bone on the upper part of the widest side of the rib, cut it off and save that as well. If you like symmetry, trim the thin end off the slab to make a slanted rectangle.

2. To skin the spareribs, use a table knife, screwdriver, or the handle of a teaspoon to push under the membrane and lift it enough for you to get a grip on it. Pull the membrane off with needlenose pliers or a wad of paper towels and discard. Removing the membrane makes for more tender ribs and allows the smoke to penetrate the meat better. It's okay if some remains.

3. Combine the pepper, salt, and granulated garlic in a small bowl to make a rub.

4. After the ribs are trimmed and skinned, rub both sides with the canola oil and sprinkle with the rub. Set aside while you build your fire.

NOTE
....
You can slow smoke the rib meat scraps, along with your ribs, for use in beans and other side dishes.

5. Fill your charcoal chimney with briquets, set the chimney on the bottom grill grate, and light, or prepare a fire in your smoker. Oil the grill grate.

6. When the coals are ready, dump them into the bottom of your grill and spread evenly across half. Scatter the wood chips on the hot coals. Place the ribs across from the coals on the indirect-heat side of the grill, racked or stacked if necessary. If your rib rack is too high for the lid to fit all the way down when ribs are racked, arrange the coals on both sides of the bottom of the grill and place the rack in the middle of the grill grate. Be sure to position the rib rack so that the rib meat is not directly above the hot coals. When the smoke starts to rise, close the lid. Place a candy thermometer in the lid vent.

7. Smoke the ribs at 225°F to 250°F (110°C to 120°C) for 4 to 6 hours, adding more briquets when necessary, or until the meat pulls away from the ends of the bone. Serve with your favorite barbecue sauce.

2 slabs 3.8 and down pork spareribs

MARINADE

½ cup (120 ml) Worcestershire sauce

2 sticks (1 cup [225 g]) unsalted butter

½ cup (120 ml) cider vinegar

1 tablespoon (18 g) garlic salt

1 teaspoon freshly ground black pepper

SMOKEHOUSE SPARERIBS

SERVES: 4 to 6

This title is just a play on words, because any and all of your barbecue pits can be called or considered your smokehouse. If you follow this recipe to the letter, you'll end up with some great smokehouse-style ribs. "Mop" means to use a dish mop to anoint the ribs with the flavored butter mixture.

....

1. Prepare the ribs by removing the membrane and trimming away any large pieces of fat.

2. Combine the remaining ingredients in a medium-size nonreactive saucepan over medium heat. Simmer until the butter has melted and the garlic salt has dissolved. Set aside to cool. Transfer half the mop to a bowl and set aside. Mop the ribs on both sides with half the mop mixture, cover with plastic wrap, and marinate for 1 hour in the refrigerator.

3. When ready to cook, prepare an indirect fire.

4. Remove the ribs from the marinade and discard the marinade. Place the ribs on the pit, cover, and cook according to the Introduction (page 6), turning and basting with the reserved marinade every 20 to 30 minutes.

5. Remove the ribs from the grill and let rest for 10 minutes before cutting into individual ribs. Serve hot.

GINGER HONEY-GLAZED BARBECUED SPARERIBS

SERVES: 4 to 6

If you like your barbecue sweet, this will do you dandy. Use clover honey because it's mild and complements rather than distracts from the overall flavor of the ribs.

....

1. To make the marinade, combine the marinade ingredients in a medium-size nonreactive saucepan and bring to a boil. Reduce the heat to medium-low and simmer for 15 minutes, stirring to blend. Remove from the heat and let cool.

2. Prepare the ribs by removing the membrane and trimming away any large pieces of fat. Place the ribs in a nonreactive baking dish or zippered-top plastic bag and pour the marinade over them. Cover with plastic wrap or seal and let marinate for at least 4 to 6 hours or overnight in the refrigerator.

3. When ready to cook, prepare an indirect fire.

4. Remove the ribs from the marinade, shaking off any excess marinade. Reserve enough of the marinade to use as a baste and transfer to a saucepan. Bring to a boil over medium-high heat; let simmer for 5 minutes, then set aside.

5. Place the ribs on the pit, cover, and cook according to the Introduction (page 6). Halfway through the cooking time, begin basting the ribs every 30 minutes with the cooked marinade.

6. While the ribs are cooking, make the glaze. Combine the glaze ingredients in a medium-size nonreactive saucepan and simmer over medium-low heat for 10 minutes, stirring. Let cool.

7. Thirty minutes before the end of the cooking time, paint the glaze all over the ribs, two or three times, turning to keep the glaze from burning or caramelizing.

8. Remove the ribs from the grill and let rest for 10 minutes before cutting into individual ribs. Serve hot.

PINEAPPLE-HONEY MARINADE

2 cups (470 ml) chicken broth

1 cup (235 ml) soy sauce

1 cup (240 g) tomato ketchup

½ cup (120 ml) pineapple juice

½ cup (170 g) clover honey

¼ cup (60 ml) cream sherry

2 tablespoons (30 g) firmly packed light brown sugar

1 teaspoon peeled and grated fresh ginger

2 cloves garlic, pressed

1 teaspoon freshly ground black pepper

1 teaspoon non-iodized salt

2 slabs 3.8 and down pork spareribs

GINGER-HONEY GLAZE

1 cup (340 g) clover honey

2 tablespoons (30 ml) soy sauce

2 teaspoons peeled and grated fresh ginger

½ teaspoon freshly ground black pepper

SWEET STUFF GLAZED BABY BACK RIBS

SERVES: 2

Baby backs are also called loin ribs since they are cut from the loin section of the pig. The bones are shorter than on spareribs and are slightly curved instead of straight. They tend to be meatier and more tender than spareribs. Prepackaged baby backs are already trimmed, saving you a preparation step. What's not to like? Contest barbecuers know the value of a good glaze on ribs, which involves brushing on a sweet barbecue sauce during the last 30 minutes of slow smoking. A glaze adds an attractive sheen to the ribs rather than a granular, crusty appearance. With the long smoking time, this is not a practical recipe for a gas grill. You can't go wrong with classic side dishes: barbecued beans, potato salad, and coleslaw.

2 full slabs baby back ribs

2 tablespoons (12 g) freshly ground black pepper

1 teaspoon fine sea salt

¾ cup (68 g) wood chips, soaked in water and drained

1 cup (235 ml) sweet, tomato-based barbecue sauce of your choice

1. To skin baby back ribs, use a table knife, screwdriver, or the handle of a teaspoon to push under the membrane and lift it enough for you to get a grip on it. Pull the membrane off with needlenose pliers or a wad of paper towels and discard. Removing the membrane makes for more tender ribs and allows the smoke to penetrate the meat better. It's okay if some remains.

2. Season the ribs with the pepper and salt and place them in your rib rack, if you are using one. Set aside.

3. Fill your charcoal chimney with briquets, set the chimney on the bottom grill grate, and light, or prepare a fire in your smoker. Oil the grill grate.

4. When the coals are ready, dump them into the bottom of your grill and spread them evenly across half. Scatter the wood chips on the hot coals. Place the ribs across from the coals on the indirect-heat side of the grill, racked or stacked if necessary. If your rib rack is too high for the lid to fit all the way down when the ribs are racked, arrange the coals on both sides of the bottom of the grill and place the rack in the middle of the grill grate. Be sure to position the rib rack so that rib meat is not directly above the hot coals. When the smoke starts to rise, close the lid. Place a candy thermometer in the lid vent.

5. Smoke the ribs at 225°F to 250°F (110°C to 120°C) for 2 to 3 hours, or until the meat pulls away from the ends of the bone. When the ribs are done, brush both sides with the barbecue sauce and return them to the indirect-heat side of the grill, close the lid, and cook for 10 to 15 minutes more, or until the glaze has set and the ribs have a sheen. Serve with extra barbecue sauce at the table.

TEX-MEX BARBECUED BABY BACK RIBS

SERVES: 4 to 6

These ribs are from south of the Red River, not south of the border. The cumin and chili powder really bring out the Tex-Mex flavor.

....

1. To make the rub, in a small bowl, combine the rub ingredients and blend well.

2. Prepare the ribs by removing the membrane and trimming away any large pieces of fat. Season the ribs on both sides with the rub.

3. Prepare an indirect fire.

4. Place the ribs on the pit, cover, and cook according to the Introduction (page 6).

5. While the ribs are cooking, make the sauce. Combine the sauce ingredients in a medium-size nonreactive saucepan. Bring to a boil, cover, reduce the heat to medium-low heat, and simmer for 15 minutes.

6. Thirty minutes before the end of the cooking time, brush the ribs on both sides with the sauce. Continue to glaze and turn to keep the sauce from burning or caramelizing.

7. Remove the ribs from the grill and let rest for 10 minutes before cutting into individual ribs. Serve hot with the remaining sauce on the side.

TEX-MEX RUB

1 tablespoon (15 g) firmly packed dark brown sugar

1 tablespoon (13 g) granulated cane sugar

1 tablespoon (8 g) chili powder

1 tablespoon (7 g) sweet Hungarian paprika

1 tablespoon (18 g) garlic salt

2 teaspoons ground cumin

2 teaspoons seasoned salt

1 teaspoon freshly ground black pepper

½ teaspoon dried oregano leaves

2 slabs baby back ribs

FINISHING AND DIPPING SAUCE

1 cup (240 g) tomato ketchup

½ cup (115 g) firmly packed dark brown sugar

¼ cup (60 ml) cider vinegar

2 tablespoons (30 ml) Worcestershire sauce

2 teaspoons dry mustard

1 teaspoon crushed red pepper

¼ teaspoon cayenne pepper

2 tablespoons (36 g) garlic salt

1 tablespoon (6 g) freshly ground black pepper

2 teaspoons celery salt

1 teaspoon onion salt

2 slabs baby back ribs

KANSAS CITY BARBECUE SAUCE

¼ cup (60 ml) canola oil

1 medium-size onion, minced

2 cloves garlic, minced

Two 6-ounce (170 g) cans tomato paste

¼ cup (60 ml) distilled white vinegar

¼ cup (60 ml) Worcestershire sauce

¼ cup (85 g) clover honey

¼ cup (60 g) firmly packed light brown sugar

2 tablespoons (22 g) prepared yellow mustard

1 tablespoon (6 g) freshly ground black pepper

2 teaspoons rubbed sage

2 teaspoons liquid smoke flavoring (optional)

1 teaspoon dried basil leaves

1 teaspoon non-iodized salt

½ teaspoon cayenne pepper

KANSAS CITY-STYLE BABY BACK RIBS

SERVES: 4 to 6

You can get these ribs only from somebody's backyard barbecue or at a barbecue contest because they don't make ribs this good at most barbecue restaurants. The seasoning, with its emphasis on celery salt, and the tomato-based barbecue sauce are what make this a Kansas City–style rib recipe.

....

1. Prepare an indirect fire.

2. Combine the garlic salt, pepper, celery salt, and onion salt in a small bowl and blend well.

3. Prepare the ribs by removing the membrane and trimming away any large pieces of fat. Season the ribs on both sides with the seasoning mix.

4. Place the ribs on the pit, cover, and cook according to the Introduction (page 6).

5. While the ribs are cooking, prepare the barbecue sauce. Heat the oil over medium-high heat in a medium-size nonreactive saucepan. Add the onion and garlic and cook, stirring, for about 2 minutes; don't let the onion brown. Stir in the tomato paste and vinegar, then blend in the remaining ingredients. Bring to a simmer, reduce the heat to medium-low, and continue to simmer for 15 minutes, stirring occasionally.

6. Thirty minutes before the end of the cooking time, brush the ribs on both sides with the sauce and continue to glaze and turn to keep the sauce from burning or caramelizing.

7. Remove the ribs from the grill and let rest for 10 minutes before cutting into individual ribs. Serve hot with the remaining barbecue sauce on the side.

SPICY COUNTRY-STYLE RIBS

SERVES: 6 to 8

This spicy country-style rub is way out of character for me, because of the granular size of the salt and sugar, but it works really well because the salt and sugar granules are the same size. Country-style ribs come from the tougher blade end of the pork loin or pork butt, which is cut into individual 1-inch (2.5 cm)-wide strips to look like ribs, so they require a long, slow smoking time of 3 to 4 hours.

....

1. To make the rub, combine the rub ingredients in a medium-size bowl and blend well. Sprinkle the rub evenly all over the ribs.

2. Prepare an indirect fire.

3. Place the ribs on the pit, cover, and cook according to the Introduction (page 6). About halfway through the cooking time, 1½ to 2 hours, start basting the ribs every 30 minutes with the apple juice. Serve hot.

SPICY COUNTRY RUB

¼ cup (48 g) raw or turbinado sugar

2 tablespoons (29 g) coarse kosher salt

1 tablespoon (18 g) garlic salt

1 tablespoon (18 g) seasoned salt

¼ cup (29 g) sweet Hungarian paprika

2 tablespoons (16 g) chili powder

2 tablespoons (12 g) coarsely ground black pepper

1 tablespoon (5 g) cayenne pepper

1 teaspoon ground ginger

1 teaspoon ground allspice

½ teaspoon ground cloves

5 pounds (2.3 kg) country-style ribs, trimmed of excess fat

2 cups (470 ml) apple juice

3 tablespoons (18 g) freshly ground black pepper

1 teaspoon fine sea salt

One 5-pound (2.3 kg) (or more) bone-in pork shoulder

2 cups (180 g) wood chips, soaked in water and drained

1 cup (235 ml) homemade or store-bought barbecue sauce (optional)

LOTSA BARK BARBECUED PORK SHOULDER

SERVES: 4

Formerly a Southern barbecue standard, barbecued pork shoulder/blade roast/butt is now popular in barbecue joints across America. Since shoulders are too thick for deep smoke penetration, they carry only a hint of smoke when barbecued. A good, crusty bark—the meat's dark crust—is prized by barbecue-shoulder aficionados. Getting a good bark on your butt involves starting out with a higher temperature, then lowering the heat for slow smoking. For true Southern pork shoulder, go with hickory wood. Because pork shoulder slow smokes for at least 6 hours, this isn't one to try on the gas grill.

1. Mix the pepper and salt together and rub it on all surfaces of the pork. Set aside while you build the fire.

2. Fill your charcoal chimney with briquets, set the chimney on the bottom grill grate, and light, or prepare a fire in your smoker. Oil the grill grate.

3. When the coals are ready, dump them into the bottom of your grill and spread them evenly across half. Scatter the wood chips on the hot coals. Place the pork on the indirect-heat side of the grill across from the coals. Increase the temperature to 350°F (180°C) by opening the bottom vents on your grill. When the smoke starts to rise, close the lid. Place a candy thermometer in the lid vent. Smoke for 30 to 45 minutes to get the bark started.

4. Reduce the temperature by closing the vents until you're at 225°F to 250°F (110°C to 120°C). Smoke the pork for 6 to 8 hours, or until tender, adding more briquets when necessary. Check for tenderness by pulling a piece of meat off and tasting it. The mark of a shoulder done to perfection is when you can remove the blade bone by pulling it out with your hand.

5. When the pork is done, set it aside in a pan for 30 minutes, then move it to a cutting board. Serve it pulled (stringy portions torn off by hand), sliced, chopped, or as a piggie sandwich (chopped or pulled pork topped with coleslaw on a bun), with sauce on the side if desired.

KOREAN-STYLE CHOPS

SERVES: 6

The traditional treatment for barbecued pork in the American South pairs the rich meat with vinegar bastes and sauces. Here we use that combo to another end. Pungent as the marinade may seem, the relatively brief soaking time leaves just a subtle spicing behind.

....

1. Approximately 2 to 3 hours before you plan to smoke the pork, combine the marinade ingredients in a bowl. Place the chops in a plastic bag or shallow nonreactive dish, pour the marinade over them, and refrigerate them for at least 1 hour.

2. Bring your smoker to its appropriate cooking temperature.

3. Remove the pork from the refrigerator and let it sit at room temperature for 30 minutes.

4. Warm a heavy skillet over high heat. Quickly sear the chops on both sides.

5. Transfer the chops to the smoker. Cook the pork to an internal temperature of 160°F (70°C), about 50 to 60 minutes at a cooking temperature of 225°F to 250°F (110°C to 120°C). Serve hot.

MARINADE

1½ cups (355 ml) white vinegar

8 cloves garlic, minced

2 tablespoons (30 ml) Thai or Vietnamese fish sauce

2 tablespoons (12 g) ground black pepper

2 tablespoons (30 ml) vegetable oil

6 bone-in, center-cut pork chops, each ¾ inch (1.9 cm) thick

Three 1½-pound (683 g)
pork tenderloins

MARINADE

2 cups (470 ml) apple juice

¼ cup (60 g) firmly packed
light brown sugar

2 tablespoons (36 g) garlic salt

1 tablespoon (7 g) sweet
Hungarian paprika

2 teaspoons onion salt

1 teaspoon celery salt

1 teaspoon dry mustard

1 teaspoon freshly ground
black pepper

APPLE-SMOKED APPLE-BASTED PORK TENDERLOIN

SERVES: 4 to 6

Trim off all the silverskin, a shiny membrane, from the tenderloin with
a sharp paring or boning knife. If you've only had grilled pork tenderloin,
experiment with this recipe. Apple wood–smoked pork tenderloin is
wonderful. Add the apple wood chunks to the coals when you start
cooking and when you add more hot coals. Serve with your favorite
barbecue sauce on the side.

1. Trim the fat and silverskin from the tenderloins, place them in a
zippered-top plastic bag, add the apple juice, and let marinate in the
refrigerator for 2 hours.

2. Combine the remaining ingredients in a small bowl and blend well.

3. When ready to cook, prepare an indirect fire and throw 3 chunks of
apple wood on the coals.

4. Remove the tenderloins from the marinade. Transfer the remaining
marinade to a saucepan and bring to a boil over medium-high heat; let
simmer for 5 minutes, then set aside. Sprinkle the tenderloins evenly with
the sugar-and-spice mixture.

5. Set the tenderloins on the pit, cover, and smoke at 230°F to 250°F
(110°C to 120°C) for 1½ to 2 hours, basting with the cooked reserved
marinade after 1 hour of cooking. Baste and turn the tenderloins every
30 minutes. Tenderloins are done when an instant-read meat thermometer
inserted into the center registers at least 145°F (60°C); if you like your
pork more done, then aim for 155°F to 165°F (65°C to 75°C).

6. Let the pork tenderloins rest for 10 minutes before slicing.

ANCHO AND CHIPOTLE-RUBBED SMOKED PORK LOIN

SERVES: 8 to 12

This pork loin is not for the faint of heart. The chiles add mucho gusto and liven up those taste buds. For the best flavor, let the pork loin marinate for at least 6 to 8 hours or overnight in the refrigerator.

....

1. Place both dried chiles in a preheated 200°F (100°C or gas mark ¼) oven for 3 to 4 minutes. Remove the chiles, let cool, and, wearing rubber gloves, open them up. Remove the stems and seeds. Place the chiles in a heat-resistant bowl and cover them with boiling water. When they are soft, which takes about 15 minutes, drain and place in a blender or food processor fitted with a steel blade. Add the onion, garlic, lard, toasted cumin seeds, salt, black pepper, and cloves and pulse on and off until you have a rough paste. Wearing rubber gloves, rub the paste all over the pork loin. Place in a nonreactive baking dish or large zippered-top plastic bag, cover with plastic wrap or seal, and let marinate in the refrigerator for at least 6 to 8 hours or overnight.

2. When ready to cook, prepare an indirect fire.

3. Place the pork on the pit, cover, and smoke at 230°F to 250°F (110°C to 120°C). Turn and rotate the loin after about 1½ hours. Continue to smoke until an instant-read meat thermometer inserted into the center registers 145°F (60°C), 3 to 4 hours total; if you like your pork more done, then aim for 155°F to 165°F (65°C to 75°C).

4. Let the pork loin rest for 10 minutes before slicing. Serve sliced with the salsa of your choice.

ANCHO AND CHIPOTLE RUB

3 dried chipotle chiles

2 dried ancho chiles

Boiling water, as needed

¼ cup (24 g) grated onion

1 tablespoon (15 g) minced garlic

2 tablespoons (28 g) lard (vegetable oil may be substituted, but it is not recommended)

1 tablespoon (6 g) cumin seeds, toasted in a dry skillet over medium heat until fragrant, then ground

2 teaspoons fine sea salt

1 teaspoon freshly ground black pepper

½ teaspoon ground cloves

One 5- to 6-pound (2.3 to 2.7 kg) boneless pork loin, trimmed of excess fat

Salsa or peach chipotle salsa

SWEET AND HOT SPICE RUB

2 tablespoons (26 g) granulated cane sugar

2 tablespoons (30 g) firmly packed dark brown sugar

2 tablespoons (14 g) sweet Hungarian paprika

2 tablespoons (36 g) garlic salt

1 tablespoon (18 g) onion salt

1 tablespoon (8 g) chili powder

1 tablespoon (6 g) freshly ground black pepper

2 teaspoons seasoned salt

1 teaspoon celery salt

1 teaspoon ground ginger

½ teaspoon ground allspice

¼ teaspoon ground cloves

¼ teaspoon dried rosemary leaves

One 9- to 12-rib pork loin crown roast

Apple juice as needed

SMOKED SWEET AND HOT CROWN OF PORK

SERVES: 8 to 12

Crown of pork is a great cut of meat for a party meal; it's delicious, makes a wonderful show, and is not hard to cook. A crown roast—basically a string of loin chops that are tied together in a circle to form a crown— must be ordered in advance from a butcher. Make sure the butcher ties it securely. Apple wood is great to use on the pit for this recipe.

1. Prepare an indirect fire.

2. To make the rub, combine all the rub ingredients in a medium-size bowl and blend well. Sprinkle the roast evenly all over with the rub. Cover the pork bones with aluminum foil to keep them from browning.

3. Place the roast on the pit, cover, and smoke at 230°F to 250°F (110°C to 120°C) for about 2 hours, basting with apple juice after the first hour of cooking. Rotate the roast 180 degrees, baste, and cook for 2 hours longer, basting every hour. Rotate another 180 degrees, baste, and cook until an instant-read meat thermometer inserted into the center away from any bone registers 145°F (60°C), about 1 hour longer. If you like your pork more done, then aim for 155°F to 165°F (65°C to 75°C).

4. Untie the roast and remove the foil. Let the pork rest for 10 minutes before slicing.

APPLE-SMOKED PORK BUTT WITH SWEET GARLIC RUB

SERVES: 8 to 10

Pork smoked with apple wood is a great flavor combination you will enjoy. Apple wood gives a lighter smoke and is less harsh than hickory or mesquite over a long smoking time. Add the apple wood chunks to the coals when you start cooking and when you add more hot coals.

1. Prepare an indirect fire.

2. To make the rub, combine the rub ingredients in a small bowl and blend well.

3. Brush the prepared mustard lightly over the entire pork butt. Sprinkle the rub evenly all over the pork butt.

4. Place the pork on the pit, cover, and cook according to the Introduction (page 6), adding apple wood chunks. Baste with the apple juice when you turn the meat the first time, then baste every hour or when you replenish your fire.

5. If you want to slice the butt, cook it until an instant-read meat thermometer inserted into the center registers 165°F to 185°F (75°C to 85°C). Let it rest for 10 to 15 minutes, then remove the bone and slice it. If you want to pull and chop the butt, cook it to an internal temperature of 190°F to 205°F (90°C to 100°C). The bone should just pull out cleanly. Let it rest for 10 to 15 minutes, then put it on a cutting board and cut or chop into the desired pieces. You can also use two forks to shred the pork if you want.

6. To serve pork butt, you can slice it, dice it, or shred it. Put the pieces in a bowl or on a plate, mix 1 cup (235 ml) barbecue sauce with ¼ to ½ cup (60 to 120 ml) distilled white or cider vinegar and maybe a little bit of rub, and pour this mixture over the pork. Then toss it to blend and serve.

SWEET GARLIC RUB

¼ cup (50 g) granulated cane sugar

2 tablespoons (36 g) garlic salt

2 tablespoons (36 g) seasoned salt

2 tablespoons (14 g) sweet Hungarian paprika

1 tablespoon (8 g) chili powder

1 tablespoon (6 g) freshly ground black pepper

1 teaspoon dry mustard

½ teaspoon cayenne pepper

½ teaspoon ground ginger

¼ cup (44 g) prepared yellow mustard

One 5-pound (2.3 kg) bone-in Boston pork butt, trimmed

4 cups (940 ml) apple juice as needed

3

SMOKY BEEF
AND LAMB

BRAGGIN' RIGHTS BRISKET

SERVES: 8

Slow smoking a beef brisket until tender and flavorful takes time and patience. If, after hours of cooking, your brisket is still tough, don't be discouraged. Most likely it didn't cook long enough or it was cooked at a temperature that was too high and it got too dry.

To start, buy a whole, untrimmed brisket. Untrimmed is important, because fat is essential for a tender brisket. Second, don't try any fancy marinade, rub, or baste until you've cooked a brisket with this simple salt-and-pepper rub. After that, jazzier rubs and/or bastes are your choice. Third, be prepared: You'll need at least 10 pounds (4.5 kg) of charcoal briquets and a lot of vigilance in managing the temperature to see you through to the end. A 10-pound (4.5 kg) brisket can take up to 12 hours to cook. Larger briskets take as long as 15 to 20 hours. The rule of thumb is 1½ to 2 hours of slow-smoking time per pound of meat. The brisket will be done way before it's tender. And don't even think about using a gas grill! Seasoned boiled red potatoes, smashed and mixed with smoke-roasted garlic, and a grilled vegetable medley make good sides.

....

1. Fill your charcoal chimney with briquets, set the chimney on the bottom grill grate, and light, or prepare a fire in your smoker. Oil the grill grate. Sprinkle the brisket with the salt and pepper.

2. When the coals are ready, dump them into the bottom of your grill and spread them evenly across half. Scatter the wood chips on the hot coals. Place the brisket, fat side up, on the indirect-heat side. When the smoke starts to rise, close the lid. Place a candy thermometer in the lid vent of a charcoal grill or smoker. Control the temperature by opening and closing the bottom vents. To raise the temperature, open the vents more; to cool things down, close the vents a bit.

One 8- to 10-pound
(3.5 to 4.5 kg) brisket

2 tablespoons (29 g)
fine sea salt

¼ cup (34 g) freshly ground
black pepper

1 cup (90 g) wood chips,
soaked in water and drained

NOTE

Some kettle grills will go 4 to 6 hours before needing more coals. Each cooker—even the same brand and model—is different. Get to know yours.

3. Smoke the brisket at 225°F to 250°F (110°C to 120°C), adding more briquets (but not wood) at 3- to 4-hour intervals or whenever required to keep the temperature constant (see Note). Plan on smoking the brisket for 10 to 12 hours or until a meat thermometer inserted into the thickest part registers 165°F (75°C) and a meat fork inserted into the center and given a twist will shred the meat. (Many cooks wrap the brisket in aluminum foil after 6 to 8 hours and leave it in foil for the duration of the cooking time, a technique called the "Texas Crutch," but some say the foil turns the brisket into "pot roast." Learn how to cook a brisket without foil and you'll never need or want to try it with foil.)

4. Trim the excess fat before slicing the meat. Separate the lower brisket flat from the upper point. Cut the meat against the grain. Texans like thick slices. Kansas Citians like thin slices.

4 pounds (1.75 kg) meaty
short ribs

OLIVE OIL BASTE

½ cup to 1 cup (120 to 235 ml)
extra-virgin olive oil, as desired

2 tablespoons (12 g) freshly
ground black pepper

1 teaspoon fine sea salt

½ teaspoon granulated garlic

1 cup (90 g) wood chips,
soaked in water and drained

Tomato-based barbecue sauce
for serving

BARBECUED SHORT RIBS WITH OLIVE OIL BASTE

SERVES: 4

Some barbecuers use a baste as a matter of course—melted butter or oil
blended with flavorings such as honey, black coffee, or fruit juice. The
purpose of a baste is to keep food moist during low-and-slow smoking,
whereas a liquid concoction called a mop is brushed onto the meat like a
baste, but instead is used to take away some of the fat that comes to the
surface as the meat cooks.

For this recipe, choose thick and meaty short ribs, one or two per serving,
depending upon the size of the ribs and the appetites of your guests.
Seasoned pinto beans and a colorful slaw make excellent side dishes.

1. Fill your charcoal chimney with briquets, set the chimney on the
bottom grill grate, and light, or prepare a fire in your smoker. For a gas
grill, turn half the burners to high. Oil the grill grate. Using a paring knife
or needlenose pliers, strip the membrane from the bone side of the
ribs. Brush the ribs with half of the olive oil, and sprinkle lightly with the
pepper, salt, and granulated garlic.

2. When the coals are ready, dump them into the bottom of your grill and
spread them evenly across half. Scatter the wood chips on the hot coals
or place them in a metal container as close as possible to a burner on a
gas grill. Place the ribs, bone side down, on the indirect-heat side. When
the smoke starts to rise, close the lid. Place a candy thermometer in the
lid vent of a charcoal grill or smoker.

3. Smoke the ribs at 225°F to 250°F (110°C to 120°C) for 45 to 60 minutes,
or until the meat has pulled away from the bone, brushing them with the
remaining olive oil after the first half hour. For a crusty bark (also known
as a crust or coating), first grill both the meaty and bone sides directly
over coals or flames for 5 minutes each, then move the ribs to the
indirect-heat side to finish smoking. Remove the ribs from the grill and
let rest, covered, for 15 minutes. Serve with a tomato-based barbecue
sauce on the side.

SMOKED PRIME RIB

SERVES: 6 to 8

The most difficult part of cooking a standing rib roast is paying for it. Save it for special occasions when you have something big to celebrate but don't have all day to cook. Once you've slow-smoked a standing rib roast, you'll never put one in the oven again. This recipe features a simple slather, which is a mixture of flavorings (usually without sweeteners) that you can brush on the exterior of the meat to keep it moist and help it get a good bark (also known as a crust or coating). Some examples of simple slathers are American mustard over a pork butt or a combination of Dijon mustard and mayonnaise over a salmon fillet to be smoked. For a robust rib roast, use a heavier wood-smoke flavor like mesquite, or get a medium smoke flavor from pecan, apple, cherry, oak, or hickory wood. This rib roast smokes for 3 hours, so it's better to cook this on a charcoal grill/smoker or water smoker than a gas grill.

1/4 cup (60 ml) extra-virgin olive oil

1 tablespoon (6 g) freshly ground black pepper

1 tablespoon (6 g) granulated garlic

1/2 teaspoon fine sea salt

One 3-pound (1.4 kg) standing rib roast, ribs cut away from the bones, attached at the wide end, and secured with string

1/2 cup (45 g) mesquite or 1 cup (90 g) other wood chips, soaked in water and drained

1. Fill your charcoal chimney with briquets, set the chimney on the bottom grill grate, and light, or prepare a fire in your smoker. Oil the grill grate. In a bowl, combine the olive oil, pepper, granulated garlic, and salt and stir to blend. Use your hands or a basting brush to slather the rib roast with this mixture.

2. When the coals are ready, dump them into the bottom of your grill and spread them evenly across half. Scatter the wood chips on the hot coals. Place the roast, fat side up, on the indirect-heat side. When the smoke starts to rise, close the lid. Place a candy thermometer in the lid vent of a charcoal grill or smoker.

3. Smoke the ribs at 225°F to 250°F (110°C to 120°C). After 2 hours, add more coals if necessary. At this point, using clean welder's gloves or long-handled tongs, turn the roast completely around so that the opposite side is closest to the coals. Close the lid and cook for 1 more hour. After 3 hours, the roast should be tender and juicy, slightly beyond medium rare, about 140°F (60°C). When it has reached your desired level of doneness, remove it from the smoker and let it sit for 15 minutes before slicing. Slice the rib bones off first before slicing meat portions.

One 4-pound (1.8 kg) whole beef tenderloin, trimmed

2 tablespoons (30 ml) extra-virgin olive oil

Fine sea salt and freshly ground black pepper

½ cup (45 g) mesquite or 1 cup (90 g) other wood chips, soaked in water and drained

GRILLED 'N' SMOKED BEEF TENDERLOIN

SERVES: 8

Marked from the grill but with a savory scent of smoke, this beef tenderloin is king of the special occasion. And, happily for the barbecuer with an indirect fire, you can get both from the same piece of equipment. This technique also works well for pork tenderloin or lamb loin. Grill directly over the hot coals to get some good grill marks on the exterior of the meat, then place it on the indirect-heat side, add the wood chips, and smoke. Keep it simple with seasonings so you can really taste the smoke. Beef tenderloin is milder in flavor than beefier brisket, so a little mesquite smoke will go a long way. Pecan, cherry, apple, hickory, or oak will also work. Serve this with grilled or steamed asparagus and homemade mashed potatoes. The longer smoking time—at least 2 hours—makes smoking this on a gas grill impractical.

1. Fill your charcoal chimney with briquets, set the chimney on the bottom grill grate, and light, or prepare a fire in your smoker. Oil the grill grate. Brush the beef with the olive oil; sprinkle lightly with salt and pepper.

2. When the coals are ready, dump them into the bottom of your grill and spread them evenly across half. Place the tenderloin directly over the coals and grill, turning every 1 to 2 minutes, until you have good grill marks all over. Transfer the meat to the indirect-heat side.

3. Scatter the wood chips on the hot coals. When the smoke starts to rise, close the lid. Place a candy thermometer in the lid vent of a charcoal grill or smoker.

4. Smoke the tenderloin at 225°F to 250°F (110°C to 120°C) for 2½ to 3 hours, until the meat registers 135°F (55°C) for rare or to your desired doneness. Remove from the grill and let rest, covered, for 15 minutes before carving.

SMOKED BEEF TENDERLOIN WITH TOMATO–HORSERADISH SAUCE

SERVES: 8 to 10

This recipe is an elegant dinner party in the making. Try adding apple wood chunks to the fire; they'll bring out the great flavor of the beef.

....

1. Prepare an indirect fire.

2. Rub the tenderloin all over with the olive oil, then sprinkle evenly with the garlic salt and pepper.

3. Place the tenderloin on the pit, cover, and smoke at 230°F to 250°F (110°C to 120°C) until an instant-read meat thermometer is inserted into the thickest part registers between 130°F and 135°F (54.5°C to 57°C) for medium rare, about 3½ hours, or to your desired degree of doneness.

4. Remove from the pit and let cool to room temperature. To serve, slice the tenderloin thinly. Arrange on a large serving platter and serve with the sauce on the side.

One 3- to 4-pound (1.4 to 1.8 kg) beef tenderloin, trimmed of any fat and silverskin

1 tablespoon (15 ml) extra virgin olive oil

1 tablespoon (18 g) garlic salt

1 tablespoon (6 g) freshly ground black pepper

1 recipe Tomato-Horseradish Sauce (opposite)

TOMATO-HORSERADISH SAUCE

This is a colorful sauce that's great with smoked tenderloin or smoked shellfish.

MAKES: 2 cups (470 ml)

½ cup (125 g) tomato purée

½ cup (52 g) peeled, seeded, and minced cucumber

¼ cup (28 g) seeded and minced green bell pepper

¼ cup (28 g) seeded and minced red bell pepper

¼ cup (28 g) minced red onion

2 tablespoons (12 g) thinly sliced green onions (green and white parts)

1 tablespoon (10 g) grated carrot

1 tablespoon (13 g) granulated cane sugar

1 teaspoon minced mixed fresh basil, tarragon, and thyme leaves

1 teaspoon peeled and grated fresh horseradish

2 cloves garlic, pressed

1 teaspoon non-iodized salt

½ teaspoon white pepper

½ teaspoon cayenne pepper

....

Combine all the ingredients in a medium-size bowl and blend well. Cover with plastic wrap and refrigerate for at least 8 hours or, better yet, overnight to allow the flavors to blend. Serve cold or at room temperature.

HORSERADISH PASTE

1 cup (240 g) peeled and grated fresh horseradish

½ cup (120 ml) olive oil

¼ cup (38 g) cloves garlic, pressed or minced

¼ cup (75 g) kosher salt

¼ cup (24 g) cracked black peppercorns

2 tablespoons (30 g) firmly packed dark brown sugar

2 tablespoons (12 g) cumin seeds, toasted in a dry skillet over medium heat until fragrant, then ground

1 tablespoon (11 g) spicy brown mustard

One 12-pound (5.4 kg) lip-on ribeye roast, trimmed of excess fat

BARBECUED LIP-ON RIBEYE WITH HORSERADISH PASTE

SERVES: 12 to 16

A lip-on ribeye is a boneless prime rib or standing rib roast. These boneless roasts weigh between 9 and 14 pounds (4.1 and 6.4 kg), as compared to a prime rib roast, with the rib bones in, which weighs 18 to 22 pounds (8.2 to 10 kg). This recipe is great to do for a Super Bowl party.

....

1. Prepare an indirect fire.

2. To make the paste, combine the paste ingredients in a medium-size bowl and blend well with a wire whisk.

3. Place the roast on a baking sheet and rub the paste all over the roast.

4. Place the roast on the pit, cover, and cook at 230°F to 250°F (110°C to 120°C) until an instant-read meat thermometer inserted into the thickest part registers between 130°F and 135°F (54.5°C to 57°C) for medium rare, 4 to 6 hours, or to your desired degree of doneness.

5. Let rest for 15 minutes before slicing.

SMOKED DINOSAUR BONES

SERVES: 4 to 6

These huge beef ribs, the equivalent of spareribs on a hog, are delicious and fun. One rib can be a meal, though. A slab of pork spareribs weighs 3 to 4 pounds (1.4 to 1.8 kg). A slab of beef ribs weighs 7 to 8 pounds (3.3 to 3.5 kg), so you can see that these Dinosaur Bones are gigantic compared to what most people expect. The trick with beef ribs is to get them tender, so low and slow is the way to go.

Two 7- to 8-pound (3.2 to 3.5 kg) slabs beef back ribs

3 cups (705 ml) Beefy Mop Sauce (opposite)

½ cup (125 g) Jersey Beef Mustard Slather (opposite)

1 cup (100 g) beef rub

....

1. Peel off the membrane from the back of the ribs and trim away any fat clinging to the bones. A long, thin knife is best for this job. Then take a sharp pointed knife, such as a paring knife, and outline the bones with the point of the knife, cutting into the meat about ¹⁄₁₆ to ⅛ inch (1.6 to 3.2 mm).

2. Place the ribs in a shallow nonreactive baking dish or zippered-top plastic bags, if they will fit. Pour the mop sauce over the ribs, coating them, cover with plastic wrap or seal, and let marinate for at least 3 to 4 hours or overnight in the refrigerator.

3. Prepare an indirect fire.

4. Remove the ribs from the mop, reserving the excess. Pat the ribs dry with a paper towel. Transfer the mop to a small saucepan, bring to a boil, and let simmer for 5 minutes. Set aside.

5. Coat the rib bones with the mustard slather and sprinkle evenly with the rub. Turn the ribs over and repeat the process. Place the ribs on the pit, cover, and cook until tender, 4 to 6 hours. Baste with the reserved mop sauce frequently after the ribs have cooked for 1½ hours. The ribs are done when they seem tender when pierced with a knife.

BEEFY MOP SAUCE

MAKES: About 3 cups (705 ml)

2 cups (470 ml) beef broth

½ cup (120 ml) canola oil

½ cup (120 ml) Worcestershire sauce

¼ cup (60 ml) fresh lemon juice (about 2 lemons)

¼ cup (60 ml) cider vinegar

1 tablespoon (15 g) firmly packed light brown sugar

1 tablespoon (20 g) kosher salt

2 teaspoons dry mustard

1 teaspoon freshly ground black pepper

1 teaspoon granulated garlic

1 teaspoon chili powder

1 teaspoon Louisiana hot sauce

....

1. Combine all the ingredients in a medium-size nonreactive saucepan over medium heat, stirring until the sugar and spices have dissolved. Let simmer for about 10 minutes.

2. Let the sauce cool to warm or room temperature before basting.

JERSEY BEEF MUSTARD SLATHER

MAKES: About 4 cups (1 kg)

3 cups (528 g) prepared yellow mustard

¼ cup (60 ml) Worcestershire sauce

¼ cup (60 ml) Madeira wine

3 tablespoons (54 g) smoked garlic paste

1 tablespoon (15 g) firmly packed light brown sugar

1 tablespoon (6 g) finely ground black pepper

1 teaspoon fine sea salt

1 stick (½ cup [112 g]) unsalted butter, melted

....

Combine all the ingredients, except the butter, in a large nonreactive bowl and blend with an electric mixer until smooth. Add the melted butter in a slow stream while blending. Paint thinly over your meat before seasoning and cooking it.

DRY RUB

1 tablespoon (6 g)
ground black pepper

2 teaspoons dried oregano

1½ teaspoons coarse salt

¼ teaspoon cayenne

Four 1-pound (454 g) boneless
top sirloin steaks, each about
1 inch (2.5 cm) thick

CHIMICHURRI SAUCE

1 cup (60 g) minced fresh
parsley, preferably the
flat-leaf variety

½ cup (30 g) minced
fresh oregano

3 tablespoons (18 g)
minced onion

3 cloves garlic, minced

¾ cup (175 ml) extra-virgin
olive oil

2 tablespoons (30 ml)
red wine vinegar

1 teaspoon coarse salt

¼ teaspoon cayenne

CHIMICHURRI SIRLOIN

SERVES: 4

As Argentinean as the country's cowboy, the gaucho, chimichurri sauce resembles a New World pesto. The robust blend pairs perfectly with the homeland's abundant beef.

1. At least 2 hours and up to the night before you plan to smoke the sirloin, combine the dry rub ingredients together in a small bowl. Rub the steaks well with the mixture, wrap them in plastic, and refrigerate them for at least 1½ hours.

2. Make the chimichurri, stirring together the ingredients in a small bowl. Refrigerate the sauce until needed.

3. Bring your smoker to its appropriate cooking temperature.

4. Remove the steaks from the refrigerator and let them sit at room temperature for 30 minutes.

5. In a heavy skillet, sear the sirloins quickly over high heat.

6. Transfer the steaks to the smoker and cook to your desired doneness. Most people prefer the meat medium rare, when the internal temperature reaches 145°F to 150°F (60°C to 65°C), which takes about 50 to 60 minutes at a cooking temperature of 225°F to 250°F (110°C to 120°C).

7. Serve the steaks hot, accompanied with the sauce.

CHIPOTLE-HONEY FLANK STEAK

SERVES: 6 to 8

Few meats take to smoke cooking better than flank steak. The broad surfaces absorb seasoning well from rubs, pastes, and marinades, and are equally good at engulfing a copious amount of smoke in a relatively brief cooking time.

....

1. The night before you plan to smoke the steaks, combine the marinade ingredients except the honey in a lidded jar. Place the steaks in a plastic bag or shallow dish, pour the marinade over them, and refrigerate them overnight.

2. Bring your smoker to its appropriate cooking temperature.

3. Remove the steaks from the refrigerator. Drain them and reserve the marinade. Let the steaks sit at room temperature for 25 to 30 minutes.

4. In a heavy saucepan, bring the marinade to a boil and boil vigorously for 5 to 10 minutes, until reduced by one-third. Stir in the honey and heat through. Keep the mixture warm for glazing the meat.

5. Brush the steaks thickly with the glaze and transfer them to the smoker. Cook the steaks to rare or medium rare, about 35 to 45 minutes, at a temperature of 225°F to 250°F (110°C to 120°C). Remove the steaks from the smoker and brush them again with the glaze.

6. Let the steaks sit 5 minutes before slicing them thin across the grain. Serve the slices with additional glaze on the top or on the side, along with the cilantro.

MARINADE AND GLAZE

1½ cups (355 ml) tangerine or orange juice

½ cup (120 ml) fresh lime juice

¼ cup (60 ml) red wine vinegar

4 canned chipotle chiles in adobo sauce, minced, plus 2 tablespoons (30 ml) adobo sauce

2 tablespoons (30 ml) Worcestershire sauce

1½ tablespoons (25 ml) vegetable oil

2 cloves garlic, minced

1 teaspoon ground cumin

¼ cup (85 g) honey

Two 1¼-pound (567 g) flank steaks

Minced fresh cilantro, for garnish

HERB-CRUSTED BARBECUED RACK OF LAMB WITH ROASTED GARLIC SAUCE

SERVES: 4 to 8

This dish is what you order at the fancy restaurants for $40 USD per person.

....

1. Prepare an indirect fire.

2. In a small skillet over medium heat, heat the olive oil until hot, but not smoking. Add the red pepper and garlic and cook, stirring, for about 30 seconds. Add the thyme and stir for about 15 seconds. Stir in the breadcrumbs and season with salt and pepper to taste. Remove the skillet from the heat and stir in the parsley.

3. Combine the mustard and mayonnaise in a small bowl and blend well. Spread a thin layer of the mustard mixture all over the meat of the racks and pat evenly with the herbed crumbs, but not too heavily.

4. Place the racks on the pit, cover, and cook at 230°F to 250°F (110°C to 120°C) until an instant-read meat thermometer inserted into the thickest part registers 130°F to 135°F (54.5°C to 57°C) for medium rare, 2 to 3 hours, or to your desired degree of doneness.

5. Transfer the racks to a cutting board and let rest for 10 minutes before cutting into the chops. Serve with the garlic sauce on the side.

¼ cup (60 ml) olive oil

1 teaspoon crushed red pepper

4 cloves garlic, pressed

2 teaspoons dried thyme leaves

½ cup (55 g) fresh breadcrumbs

Salt and freshly ground black pepper to taste

¼ cup (15 g) minced fresh parsley leaves

¼ cup (44 g) Dijon mustard

2 tablespoons (28 g) mayonnaise

2 racks of lamb, 7 or 8 ribs each, trimmed of fat and Frenched

1 recipe Roasted Garlic Sauce (opposite)

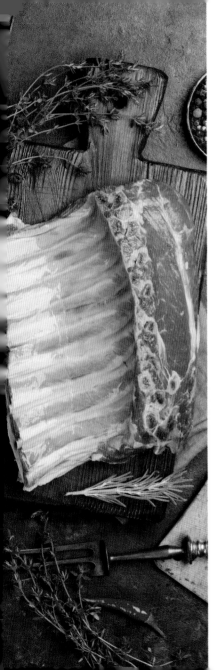

ROASTED GARLIC SAUCE

MAKES: 1 to 1½ cups (235 to 355 ml)

2 tablespoons (30 ml) olive oil, divided

1 head garlic, top cut off to expose the individual cloves

2 tablespoons (28 g) unsalted butter, divided

½ cup (50 g) chopped shallots

1 cup (235 ml) Cabernet Sauvignon

1 cup (235 ml) beef broth

¾ cup (175 ml) chicken broth

½ teaspoon kosher salt

½ teaspoon freshly ground black pepper

1. Preheat the oven to 350°F (180°C or gas mark 4).

2. Rub 1 tablespoon (15 ml) of the olive oil all over the head of garlic, place in a small baking dish, and roast in the oven until quite soft, 35 to 45 minutes. Remove from the oven and let cool. Squeeze the softened garlic from the skins and set aside.

3. Heat the remaining 1 tablespoon (15 ml) of olive oil and 1 tablespoon (14 g) of the butter in a medium-size skillet over medium heat until the butter melts. Add the shallots and cook, stirring, until golden brown, about 10 minutes. Add the wine and simmer until reduced by half. Add both broths and simmer until reduced to ¾ to 1 cup (175 to 235 ml), about 10 minutes.

4. Transfer to a blender, add the softened garlic, and process until smooth. Return the sauce to the skillet and heat to simmering. Remove from the heat, whisk in the remaining 1 tablespoon (14 g) of butter, stir in the salt and pepper, and keep warm until ready to serve.

VINEGAR MARINADE

1 cup (235 ml)
red wine vinegar

½ cup (120 ml) canola oil

2 cloves garlic, pressed

¼ cup (24 g) grated carrot

¼ cup (24 g) grated onion

1 teaspoon fine sea salt

1 teaspoon freshly ground
black pepper

½ teaspoon dried
oregano leaves

¼ teaspoon ground cloves

One 4- to 5-pound
(1.8 to 2.3 kg) boneless
leg of lamb, trimmed of fat

BEGINNER'S BARBECUED LEG OF LAMB

SERVES: 6 to 8

If you have never barbecued lamb, start with this one.

1. To make the marinade, combine the marinade ingredients in a medium-size nonreactive bowl and blend well.

2. Place the lamb in a nonreactive baking dish or a zippered-top plastic bag, pour the marinade over the lamb, coat well, cover with plastic wrap or seal, and let marinate for at least 6 to 8 hours or overnight in the refrigerator, turning several times.

3. Prepare an indirect fire.

4. Remove the lamb from the marinade, shaking off any excess. Transfer the remaining marinade to a medium-size nonreactive saucepan and bring to a boil over medium-high heat. Simmer for 5 minutes, set aside to cool, then refrigerate until ready to use.

5. Place the lamb on the pit, cover, and smoke for 2 hours at 230°F to 250°F (110°C to 120°C). Then start basting the lamb every 45 minutes with the reserved marinade. Keep checking the internal temperature in the thickest part of the leg with an instant-read meat thermometer. At 135°F to 140°F (55°C to 60°C), it should be medium rare, 3 to 4 hours total, or cook to your desired degree of doneness.

6. Let rest for 15 minutes before slicing.

4

CHICKEN, TURKEY, AND OTHER BIRDS

APPLE-SMOKED CHICKEN THIGHS

SERVES: 4

Apple smoke and apple juice spray make these chicken thighs so tasty you won't want sauce. Spraying foods with fruit juice is another trick barbecuers have in their repertoire. The sweetness in the juice counteracts the bitterness of the smoke and keeps the food moist. A fruit juice spray—usually apple or pineapple juice—is good to use on pork, chicken, or fish, of any cut or fillet, skin-on or not, bone-in or boneless. Get a plastic spray bottle from the hardware store and use it just for food purposes. Turbinado is raw sugar; if you can't find it, use light brown sugar. And here's a bonus technique—low-and-slow smoking does not make for crisp poultry skin, so right before your chicken is done, transfer it to the hot side of the grill and crisp up the skin. It's now the best of all possible worlds! Serve with potato salad and grilled or steamed fresh asparagus.

APPLE JUICE SPRAY

2 cups (470 ml) apple juice

2 tablespoons (24 g) turbinado sugar

4 large, bone-in chicken thighs, rinsed and patted dry

1 tablespoon (6 g) freshly ground black pepper

1 teaspoon fine sea salt

1 cup (90 g) wood chips, soaked in water and drained

1. To make the apple juice spray, put the juice and sugar in a stainless-steel saucepan over medium heat and cook just until the sugar is dissolved. Cool to room temperature and pour into a plastic spray bottle.

2. Sprinkle the chicken thighs with the pepper and salt. Set aside while you build the fire.

3. Fill your charcoal chimney with briquets, set the chimney on the bottom grill grate, and light, or prepare a fire in your smoker. Oil the grill grate.

4. When the coals are ready, dump them into the bottom of your grill and spread them evenly across half. Replace the grill grate. Scatter the wood chips on the hot coals. Place the chicken thighs on the indirect-heat side of the grill across from the coals and spray them with the apple juice mixture. When the smoke starts to rise, close the lid. Place a candy thermometer in the lid vent.

5. Smoke the thighs at 225°F to 250°F (110°C to 120°C) for 1 hour, spraying the chicken every 20 minutes and re-lidding the smoker. After 1 hour, spray the chicken again, then transfer to the direct-heat side and grill over hot coals for 2 minutes, turning as necessary, or until the skin has crisped all over.

SWEET AND HOT RUB

½ cup (100 g) granulated cane sugar

2 tablespoons (36 g) garlic salt

2 tablespoons (36 g) seasoned salt

2 tablespoons (14 g) sweet Hungarian paprika

1 tablespoon (7 g) chili seasoning

1 tablespoon (6 g) freshly ground black pepper

1 teaspoon ground ginger

½ teaspoon ground allspice

¼ teaspoon ground mace

4 pounds (1.8 kg) chicken wings (about 20)

1 cup (235 ml) apple juice (optional)

SWEET AND HOT BARBECUED CHICKEN WINGS

SERVES: 6 to 8

These wings have a little sweet and a little fire! When cooking chicken wings, depending on the distance between the rungs of your grill rack, you may have to cover it with a perforated grill rack. For bigger rigs, you can use a piece of expanded metal mesh, which you can get at most good hardware stores.

1. Prepare an indirect fire.

2. To make the rub, combine the rub ingredients in a small bowl and blend well.

3. Rinse the chicken wings under cold running water and pat dry with paper towels. Season evenly with the rub. Place the chicken on the pit, cover, and cook at 230°F to 250°F (110°C to 120°C), turning every 40 to 45 minutes and basting once with apple juice, if desired, until cooked through, about 2 hours.

SLATHERED AND RUBBED BARBECUED CHICKEN BREASTS

SERVES: 6

This Dijon and Italian seasoning makes for a tasty cross-cultural twist.

....

1. Rinse the chicken and pat dry with paper towels. Using a pastry brush, paint the mustard all over the chicken breasts. Season evenly with the Italian seasoning, garlic salt, and pepper. Cover with plastic wrap and let rest for 30 minutes at room temperature or up to 4 hours in the refrigerator.

2. Prepare an indirect fire.

3. Place the chicken on the pit, cover, and cook at 230°F to 250°F (110°C to 120°C) for 1½ hours. Turn and baste once with the apple juice, if desired. Continue to cook for 1½ to 3 more hours, until cooked through.

3 whole bone-in chicken breasts, halved

1 cup (176 g) Dijon mustard

2 to 3 tablespoons (17 to 25 g) Italian seasoning, to your taste

2 tablespoons (36 g) garlic salt

1 tablespoon (6 g) freshly ground black pepper

1 cup (235 ml) apple juice (optional)

HONEY SMOKED CHICKEN

SERVES: 4 to 8

This is Momma's favorite.

....

1. Rinse the chicken under cold running water and pat dry with paper towels. Place each chicken in a zippered-top plastic bag and pour 1 cup (235 ml) of the Italian marinade into each bag. Turn to coat, seal, and let marinate in the refrigerator for at least 4 hours or overnight.

2. Combine the barbecue sauce, honey, soy sauce, whiskey, and sage in a medium-size nonreactive saucepan over medium heat and simmer until well blended, about 15 minutes. Set aside.

3. Prepare an indirect fire.

4. Remove the chicken from the marinade, place rib side down on the pit, cover, and cook at 230°F to 250°F (110°C to 120°C) for 3½ to 4 hours, basting once with the apple juice, if desired, until an instant-read meat thermometer inserted into a thigh, away from the bone, registers 165°F (75°C). During the last 30 minutes of cooking, increase the heat of the fire to about 350°F (180°C) and glaze with the reserved barbecue sauce, turning every 10 minutes, until well glazed. Be careful not to caramelize (that means incinerate) the sauce.

Two 4- to 5-pound (1.8 to 2.3 kg) chickens, split in half along the backbone

2 cups (470 ml) Spicy Italian Marinade (opposite)

2 cups (470 ml) barbecue sauce of your choice

½ cup (170 g) clover honey

¼ cup (60 ml) soy sauce

¼ cup (60 ml) Jack Daniel's Sour Mash Whiskey

2 teaspoons rubbed sage

1 cup (235 ml) apple juice (optional)

SPICY ITALIAN MARINADE

MAKES: About 3 cups (705 ml)

2 cups (470 ml) canola oil

1 cup (235 ml) distilled white vinegar

¼ cup (60 ml) water

¼ cup (24 g) grated onion

1 tablespoon (3.6 g) crushed red pepper

1 tablespoon (2 g) dried basil leaves

1 tablespoon (1 g) dried parsley flakes

2 teaspoons garlic paste

¼ teaspoon white pepper

In a medium-size nonreactive bowl, whisk together the canola oil and vinegar until the mixture thickens. Add the remaining ingredients and mix until well blended.

CRANBERRY–WHISKEY MOP

2 cups (470 ml) cranberry juice

½ cup (170 g) honey

⅓ cup (80 ml) whiskey

1 tablespoon (6 g) granulated garlic

1 tablespoon (6 g) freshly ground black pepper

1 teaspoon ground sage

1 teaspoon fine sea salt

One 9- to 14-pound (4 to 6.4 kg) turkey, giblets and neck removed, rinsed, and patted dry

1 cup (90 g) wood chips, soaked in water and drained (if using Jack Daniel's wood chips, soak only 15 minutes)

NOTE

A grill mop is a small utensil consisting of a handle and a cotton or silicone brush head used for applying basting liquids to foods while grilling. They're easy to find at your local supermarket or online.

SMOKED TURKEY WITH CRANBERRY–WHISKEY MOP

SERVES: 8 or more

Barbecued turkey, fresh from the pit, makes a wonderful feast, and the leftovers are great in sandwiches and a variety of tasty casseroles. The secret to moist turkey is to mop it with a sweet/tart mixture like cranberry-whiskey mop, which you apply with a cotton dish mop or grill mop or a clean cloth.

To match the flavor, why not try wood smoke from oak barrels that have aged whiskey in them, such as Jack Daniel's whiskey-barrel wood chips? You need to soak for only about 15 minutes, as you don't want all that essence to leach out. If you can't find those, then apple, hickory, or pecan will still produce a fine, fine bird. Since the turkey smokes for 6 to 8 hours, this recipe is not for your gas grill. Serve with roasted sweet potatoes, fresh grilled or steamed and buttered green beans, and corn bread stuffing.

1. To make the mop, combine the cranberry juice, honey, whiskey, granulated garlic, pepper, sage, and salt in a medium-size bowl and whisk well.

2. Fill your charcoal chimney with briquets, set the chimney on the bottom grill grate, and light, or prepare a fire in your smoker. Oil the grill grate.

3. When the coals are ready, dump them into the bottom of your grill and spread them evenly across half. Scatter the wood chips on the hot coals. Place the turkey, breast side up, on the indirect-heat side of the grill across from the coals. Using a cotton dish mop or grill mop, apply the cranberry-whiskey mop to the turkey. When the smoke starts to rise, close the lid. Place a candy thermometer in the lid vent of a charcoal grill or smoker.

4. Smoke at 225°F to 250°F (110°C to 120°C) for 6 to 7 hours, adding more briquets as necessary, and mopping the bird every hour, until a meat thermometer registers 165°F (75°C) when inserted into the thickest part of the thigh. Remove the turkey from the cooker and let rest, covered, for 15 minutes before carving. Turkey skin may be dark brown or black when the bird is fully cooked, but the meat inside will be moist and delicious.

COUNTY FAIR BARBECUED TURKEY LEGS AND THIGHS WITH CITRUS MARINADE

SERVES: 4

Barbecued turkey legs are a favorite at fairs, festivals, and cookouts across America because they take well to sit-down or walking-around dining. The secret to this recipe is long, slow marinating. The soy in the marinade will also darken the meat to give it a rich, mahogany finish. Use this recipe for legs, thighs, or a combo of the two. Plan ahead for at least 8 hours of marinating time. Serve with grilled corn on the cob and ice cream cones for dessert. This is another recipe you can do on a gas grill.

....

1. To make the marinade, combine the olive oil, soy sauce, orange juice, lemon juice, pepper, and granulated garlic in a bowl or a large zipper-top plastic bag and mix well. Add the turkey, cover or seal, and let marinate in the refrigerator for 8 hours or overnight.

2. Fill your charcoal chimney with briquets, set the chimney on the bottom grill grate, and light, or prepare a fire in your smoker. For a gas grill, turn to low or 250°F (120°C). Oil the grill grate. Remove the turkey from the marinade, discard the marinade, and pat dry.

3. When the coals are ready, dump them into the bottom of your grill and spread them evenly across half. Replace the grill grate. Scatter the wood chips on the hot coals or place them in a metal container as close as possible to a burner on a gas grill. Place the turkey on the grill grate on the indirect-heat side across from the coals. When the smoke starts to rise, close the lid. Place a candy thermometer in the lid vent of a charcoal grill or smoker.

4. Smoke at 225°F to 250°F (110°C to 120°C) for 2 hours or until a meat thermometer registers 165°F (75°C) when inserted into the thickest part of the thigh. If you want the skin to be crispy, grill it over hot coals or flames for 3 to 4 minutes. Remove the turkey from the cooker and let rest, covered, for 15 minutes before carving. Slather lightly with your favorite barbecue sauce and serve.

CITRUS MARINADE

½ cup (120 ml) extra-virgin olive oil

¼ cup (60 ml) soy sauce

¼ cup (60 ml) freshly squeezed orange juice

2 tablespoons (30 ml) freshly squeezed lemon juice

1 teaspoon freshly ground black pepper

1 teaspoon granulated garlic

4 turkey legs or thighs

1 cup (90 g) wood chips, soaked in water and drained

Barbecue sauce of your choice for serving

PEPPERED PORT WINE SAUCE

½ cup (48 g) minced onion

2 cloves garlic, pressed

2 teaspoons peeled and minced fresh ginger

2 teaspoons rainbow peppercorns, freshly ground

¼ cup (60 ml) orange juice

¼ cup (60 ml) chicken broth

2 tablespoons (30 ml) Port wine

1 tablespoon (15 ml) cider vinegar

2 to 4 tablespoons (40 to 80 g) black raspberry jam, to your taste

¼ teaspoon cayenne pepper

Four 18- to 24-ounce (510 to 680 g) Cornish hens, split in half along the backbone

SMOKED GARLIC–HERB CORNISH HENS IN ORANGE AND ALE BASTE

SERVES: 4 to 8

Remember that the marinade in this recipe is for the birds, not for your drinking pleasure.

....

1. To make the sauce, in a medium-size nonreactive saucepan, combine the sauce ingredients and cook over medium heat, stirring, until the mixture blends together. Remove from the heat and let cool.

2. Remove the giblets from the hens, rinse the hens inside and out under cold running water, and pat dry with paper towels. Place them in a shallow nonreactive baking dish or two zippered-top plastic bags and pour the cooled sauce over them. Cover with plastic wrap or seal and let marinate for 2 to 4 hours in the refrigerator.

3. Prepare a medium-hot fire in your grill.

4. Remove the hens from the sauce, reserving the sauce. Transfer the remaining sauce to a medium-size nonreactive saucepan and bring to a boil over medium-high heat; let simmer for 5 minutes, then set aside.

5. Place the hens breast side up directly over the coals, cover, and grill, turning frequently and basting with the sauce every 15 minutes, until an instant-read meat thermometer inserted into the breast and thigh, away from the bone, registers 165°F (75°C), about 1 hour total. Serve hot.

SZECHUAN SMOKED DUCK

SERVES: 2 to 4

This duck has a little heat, but it is fantastic.

....

1. To make the rub, combine the rub ingredients in a small bowl and blend well.

2. Rinse the duck inside and out under cold running water, remove the giblets and neck, and pat dry with paper towels. Rub the duck inside and out with the sesame oil, then season evenly with the rub inside and out to taste; remember, this dish is spicy.

3. Prepare an indirect fire.

4. Place the duck on the pit breast side down, cover, and cook at 230°F to 250°F (110°C to 120°C) for 2 hours. Turn the duck, baste with the marinade, and continue to cook, basting every 30 minutes, until an instant-read meat thermometer inserted into the breast and thigh, away from the bone, registers 165°F (75°C), about 4 hours total. Let rest for 15 minutes before carving.

SZECHUAN RUB

¼ cup (60 g) firmly packed dark brown sugar

2 tablespoons (28 g) Szechuan Peppercorn Salt (opposite)

1 tablespoon (18 g) garlic salt

1 tablespoon (18 g) onion salt

2 tablespoons (14 g) sweet Hungarian paprika

1 teaspoon ground ginger

1 teaspoon Chinese dry mustard

1 teaspoon cayenne pepper

½ teaspoon ground star anise

One 4- to 5-pound (1.8 to 2.3 kg) duck, trimmed of extra fat and skin

½ cup (120 ml) toasted sesame oil

1 recipe Picante Beer Marinade (opposite)

SZECHUAN PEPPERCORN SALT

MAKES: About ¼ cup (80 g)

¼ cup (75 g) coarse kosher salt or sea salt

1 tablespoon (5 g) Szechuan peppercorns

2 teaspoons Chinese five-spice powder

....

1. Heat a small, heavy dry skillet over medium heat until it is hot. Add the salt, peppercorns, and five-spice powder and dry-roast the mixture, stirring and shaking constantly, until the mixture turns very dark—but don't let it burn!

2. Pour the mixture into a small bowl to keep it from darkening even more in the still-hot pan. Remove and discard the peppercorns.

3. Store the seasoned salt in an airtight container in a cool, dark place for up to 1 year.

PICANTE BEER MARINADE

MAKES: About 2½ cups (590 ml)

One 12-ounce (355 ml) can premium beer, allowed to go flat

½ cup (120 ml) canola oil

½ cup (50 g) thinly sliced green onions (green and white parts)

¼ cup (60 ml) soy sauce

2 tablespoons (30 g) seeded and minced serrano chiles

2 tablespoons (26 g) granulated cane sugar

4 cloves garlic, pressed

1 teaspoon kosher salt

½ teaspoon cayenne pepper

....

Combine all the ingredients in a medium-size nonreactive bowl and blend well.

5

FISH IN
THE SMOKER

ALDER-SMOKED SALMON FILLET

SERVES: 6

Hot-smoked salmon is more moist and tender than the cold-smoked variety. Serve this at a weekend brunch or for a Friday night fish dinner. The leftovers make a wonderful smoked salmon spread. Alder is the traditional wood for smoking in the Pacific Northwest—it's mild, aromatic, and great with salmon. If you decide to experiment, choose a sweeter wood for smoking salmon, one that will not overpower the natural sweetness of the fish.

This hot-smoking technique works for any type of fish fillet. You can't go wrong matching a fish with a wood from its region; for example, try Southern catfish and hickory, halibut or Arctic char and alder, Florida grouper and oak, New England bluefish and maple.

One 3-pound (1.4 kg) salmon fillet, preferably skin-on

1 tablespoon (15 ml) extra-virgin olive oil

½ teaspoon fine sea salt

1 teaspoon freshly ground black pepper

½ cup (45 g) wood chips, soaked in water and drained, or 1 cup (90 g) dry wood chips for a gas grill

Fresh dill sprigs for garnish

Lemon wedges for garnish

....

1. Fill your charcoal chimney with briquets, set the chimney on the bottom grill grate, and light, or prepare a fire in your smoker. For a gas grill, turn half the burners to medium. Rub the salmon on both sides with the olive oil and sprinkle with the salt and pepper.

2. When the coals are ready, dump them into the bottom of your grill and spread them evenly across half. Scatter the drained wood chips on the hot coals, or put the dry wood chips in a metal container and place as close as possible to a burner on a gas grill. Place the salmon on the grill grate on the indirect-heat side of the grill. When the smoke starts to rise, close the lid.

3. Smoke the salmon at 225°F to 250°F (110°C to 120°C) for 45 to 60 minutes or until the fish begins to flake when tested with a fork in the thickest part and has a smoky aroma. Garnish with fresh dill and lemon wedges.

¼ cup (23 g) dry wood chips

16 jumbo shrimp in their shells

CITRUS VINAIGRETTE

½ cup (120 ml) freshly
squeezed orange juice

¼ cup (60 ml) freshly
squeezed lemon juice

Zest of 1 orange and 1 lemon

1 cup (235 ml) canola oil

2 cloves garlic, minced

2 tablespoons (22 g)
Dijon mustard

2 tablespoons (10 g) grated
Parmesan cheese

2 scallions, chopped

2 tablespoons (2.5 g) chopped
fresh flat-leaf parsley

1 pound (454 g) whole-wheat
penne, cooked according to
package directions

Chopped scallions or fresh
flat-leaf parsley for garnish

BARBECUED SHRIMP PASTA SALAD WITH CITRUS VINAIGRETTE

SERVES: 4

Smoked shrimp can be served any number of ways—with barbecue sauce in a quesadilla, with cocktail sauce as an appetizer, or in hot or cold pasta dishes. Smoking shrimp in the shell keeps the shrimp moist. You can use a hearty smoke flavor like hickory or corncobs as your "wood," which turns the shrimp a golden hue.

To smoke shrimp, you can thread the shrimp onto a skewer, arrange them in a disposable aluminum pan, or put them directly on the grill grate. You can also smoke large sea scallops or oysters on the half shell this way—cook them until they're opaque and just firm. Mussels or oysters in the shell need a higher heat to pop open; squid and octopus will get tough and are better when grilled quickly.

....

1. Fill your charcoal chimney with briquets, set the chimney on the bottom grill grate, and light, or prepare a fire in your smoker. For a gas grill, turn half the burners to high.

2. When the coals are ready, dump them into the bottom of your grill and spread them evenly across half. Scatter the wood chips on the hot coals, or place them in a metal container as close as possible to a burner on a gas grill. Place the shrimp on the grill grate on the indirect-heat side of the grill. When the smoke starts to rise, close the lid.

3. Smoke the shrimp at 350°F (180°C) for 7 to 10 minutes or until opaque. When cool enough to handle, peel and devein the shrimp. Bring the shrimp indoors while you make the pasta salad or refrigerate them until ready to serve.

4. Combine the orange and lemon juices, orange and lemon zests, canola oil, garlic, mustard, Parmesan, scallions, and parsley in a quart-size jar. Place the lid on the jar and shake to mix thoroughly. Pour the mixture on the cooked pasta and toss. To serve, arrange 4 shrimp on each serving of pasta, and garnish with the scallions or parsley.

SIMPLE SMOKED FISH FILLETS

SERVES: 6 to 8

Pecan, grapevine, or apple wood give fish a nice flavor. Smoking times will vary depending on the size and thickness of the fillets.

....

1. Prepare an indirect fire.

2. Rinse the fillets and pat them dry with paper towels. Brush both sides with the olive oil and season evenly with the salt, pepper, and Old Bay.

3. Place the fillets in a disposable aluminum pan, skin side down, place the pan on the pit, cover, and cook at 230°F to 250°F (110°C to 120°C) until the fillets flake easily and are firm to the touch, 1½ to 2 hours.

Eight 4- to 6-ounce (115 to 170 g) fish fillets, such as rockfish (striped bass), Atlantic croaker (hardhead), sea trout, or drum

½ cup (120 ml) olive oil

1 teaspoon fine sea salt

1 teaspoon freshly ground black pepper

1 teaspoon Old Bay seasoning

1½ cups (135 g) pecan chips

1½ to 2 pounds (681 to 900 g) salmon fillets, skin left on

½ cup (120 ml) olive oil

2 tablespoons (14 g) Old Bay seasoning

1 tablespoon (15 g) coarse sea salt

1 tablespoon (6 g) freshly ground black pepper

PECAN-SMOKED SALMON

SERVES: 6 to 8

While this salmon calls for pecan chips, apple and grapevine also add a nice subtle flavor.

....

1. Prepare an indirect fire. When it's ready, place the pecan chips on the coals.

2. Rinse the fish under cold running water and pat dry with paper towels. Brush the salmon on both sides with the olive oil, then season evenly on both sides with the Old Bay, salt, and pepper.

3. Place the fillets on the pit, cover, and cook at 230°F to 250°F (110°C to 120°C) until the salmon flakes easily, about 2 hours.

SWEET AND HOT SALMON STEAKS

SERVES: 4

As simple as it is sweet, this straightforward preparation embraces the essential qualities of a salmon steak.

....

1. About 1½ hours before you plan to smoke the salmon steaks, combine the paste ingredients in a small bowl. Rub the salmon steaks thoroughly with the paste, wrap them in plastic, and refrigerate them for at least 1 hour.

2. Bring your smoker to its appropriate cooking temperature.

3. Remove the salmon from the refrigerator and let it sit covered at room temperature for 15 to 20 minutes.

4. Transfer the salmon to the smoker. Smoke the steaks until just cooked through and flaky, about 45 to 55 minutes at a temperature of 225°F to 250°F (110°C to 120°C).

5. Transfer the salmon to a serving platter and serve hot or chilled.

PASTE

¼ cup (44 g) hot sweet mustard

¼ cup (24 g) minced onion

Juice of 1 lemon

2 teaspoons minced fresh dill or 1 teaspoon dried dill

1 teaspoon coarse salt

Four 7- to 8-ounce (198 to 225 g) salmon steaks, each about 1 inch (2.5 cm) thick

MUSTARD–LIME MARINADE

¼ cup (60 ml) fresh lime juice (about 4 limes)

2 tablespoons (30 ml) olive oil

1 tablespoon (11 g) Dijon mustard

1 teaspoon grated lime zest

1 teaspoon non-iodized salt

1 teaspoon finely ground black pepper

4 salmon steaks, 1 inch (2.5 cm) thick (about 1½ pounds [681 g])

⅓ cup (96 g) sesame seeds, toasted in a dry skillet over medium heat until fragrant

SMOKED MUSTARD–LIME MARINATED SALMON WITH SESAME SEEDS

SERVES: 4

If you want a little heat with this salmon, add a little crushed red pepper to the marinade. Again, this recipe calls for pecan chips for smoking salmon, but use whatever wood you prefer.

1. To make the marinade, in a shallow nonreactive baking dish, combine the marinade ingredients, blending with a wire whisk. Rinse the fish under cold running water and pat dry with paper towels. Add the fish to the marinade, turning to coat. Cover with plastic wrap and let marinate at room temperature for 30 minutes.

2. Prepare an indirect fire.

3. Remove the fish from the marinade. Transfer the remaining marinade to a nonreactive saucepan and bring to a boil over medium-high heat; simmer for 5 minutes, let cool, then refrigerate until ready to use. Sprinkle the salmon (flesh side only) evenly with the toasted sesame seeds.

4. Place the salmon on the pit, cover, and cook at 230°F to 250°F (110°C to 120°C) for 20 minutes. Baste with the reserved marinade, turn, cover, and cook until the salmon flakes easily with a fork, 20 to 40 minutes longer.

6

VEGETABLES AND BEANS IN THE SMOKER

WHOLE SMOKED GARLIC

SERVES: 4

Your guests will enjoy the fun and flavors they get from squeezing sweet, soft, smoked garlic from a clove, spreading it on a baguette slice, and topping it with a slice of goat cheese and tomato. The mere thought of it makes me hungry! Because garlic starts out pungent but then gets sweet as it slowly smokes, choose a medium-flavor wood. When preparing the garlic heads for smoking, take care to slice off only enough to make it easy to squeeze the smoked garlic from each clove. You can also use this technique with whole, cored tomatoes, small new potatoes, or stemmed mushrooms—just smoke until the vegetables are softened and have a good, smoky aroma.

4 whole heads garlic, ½ inch (1 cm) sliced off the pointed top of each

⅓ cup (30 g) wood chips, soaked in water and drained, or 1 cup (90 g) dry wood chips for a gas grill

1 whole-grain baguette, sliced

One 7½-ounce (213 g) goat cheese log

1 medium-size ripe tomato, sliced, or 8 cherry tomatoes

Fine sea salt and freshly ground black pepper

1. Fill your charcoal chimney three-quarters full with briquets, set the chimney on the bottom grill grate, and light, or prepare a fire in your smoker. For a gas grill, turn half the burners to medium. Spray a 6 × 6-inch (15 × 15 cm) piece of heavy-duty aluminum foil or a disposable aluminum pan with olive or canola oil and arrange the garlic on it.

2. When the coals are ready, dump them into the bottom of your grill and spread them evenly across half. Scatter the drained wood chips on the hot coals, or put the dry wood chips in a metal container and place as close as possible to a burner on a gas grill. Place the garlic on the indirect-heat side of the grill. When the smoke starts to rise, close the lid.

3. Smoke the garlic at 225°F to 250°F (110°C to 120°C) for 45 minutes or until it has a mild, smoky aroma. To serve, set out the smoked garlic, baguette slices, goat cheese, and tomatoes. Guests can squeeze out the smoked garlic cloves and spread them onto the bread, along with the cheese, then top with a slice of tomato and salt and pepper to taste.

SMOKE-BAKED BARBECUE CHILE PIE

SERVES: 6

Smoke baking is a great technique to use for garlic bread, pizzas, quiche, or a savory breakfast casserole—whenever you want to bake and get a hit of smoky flavor at the same time. You can smoke bake using a charcoal grill, gas grill, or traditional smoker with a smoking temperature you can control (water smokers have a set temperature of 225°F to 250°F (110°C to 120°C) and will not work for this recipe).

You can substitute other varieties of chiles (or bell peppers for a less spicy result) in this recipe and experiment with additional ingredients, such as a garnish of chopped scallions, cilantro, or parsley. A teaspoon of your favorite chili seasoning blend or barbecue dry rub could add a special accent. If you can't get Hatch chile peppers, no problem. Buy fresh green Anaheim peppers and fire roast them at home. For a true Southwestern flavor use the heavier mesquite wood—very sparingly here—or pecan. This is a great dish for a light supper or an outdoor brunch.

....

1. Fill your charcoal chimney with briquets, set the chimney on the bottom grill grate, and light, or prepare a fire in your smoker. For a gas grill, turn half the burners to high.

2. Line the bottom and sides of the pie crust with the chile pepper strips, reserving a few to garnish the top of the pie. Top with the cheese, spreading it out evenly over the bottom of the crust.

3. In a small sauté pan over medium heat, sauté the onions in the olive oil until softened, about 3 minutes. In a medium-size bowl, combine the eggs and onion, then pour the mixture over the cheese. Arrange the reserved chile pepper strips on the top of the pie.

1 frozen prepared deep-dish pie crust

8 ounces (225 g) fire-roasted mild Hatch or other chile peppers, seeded and sliced into strips of varying size (see Note)

8 ounces (58 g) shredded cheddar–Monterey Jack cheese blend

¼ cup (40 g) chopped Texas sweet or Vidalia onion

½ teaspoon olive oil

4 large eggs, beaten

¼ cup (23 g) wood chips, soaked in water and drained, or ½ cup (45 g) dry wood chips for a gas grill

4 ounces (113 g) hickory- or maple-smoked bacon, cooked until crisp and chopped

4. When the coals are ready, dump them into the bottom of your grill and spread them evenly across half. Scatter the drained wood chips on the hot coals, or put the dry wood chips in a metal container and place as close as possible to a burner on a gas grill. Place the pie on the indirect-heat side of the grill. When the smoke starts to rise, close the lid.

5. Smoke bake the pie at 350°F (180°C) for 40 to 45 minutes or until the crust has browned, the filling has set, and the pie has a mild, smoky aroma. Sprinkle with the bacon before serving.

NOTE

Fire roast the chiles by grilling them over hot coals until the skins blacken, then remove the papery skin, seeds, and membrane. (You should wear food-preparation gloves for this because the oil from hot chiles will stick to your hands. If you rub your eyes or other sensitive areas after working with the chiles, it can be painful. If the chiles are mild, however, gloves aren't necessary.)

SMOKED STUFFED CHILE PEPPERS

SERVES: 4

Chile "poppers"—just pop 'em in your mouth—are on many restaurant menus, and they're easy to prepare in your own backyard. They need to smoke at a higher temperature so the bacon wrapped around the outside of the chile gets cooked through. Although higher-heat smoking is technically not considered low-and-slow traditional barbecue, it does have its place in recipes like this one (and for people who use a ceramic smoker, which automatically smokes at a higher temperature). At a lower temperature, the bacon won't crisp up. You can also use this technique to smoke other bacon-wrapped appetizers like shrimp, water chestnuts, or green bean bundles. If you like, substitute goat cheese, garlic-and-herb cream cheese, or even pimiento cheese spread for the cream cheese and cheddar. You can also use almonds or walnuts instead of the pecans, or omit the nuts.

These poppers are so addictive that you can make a meal out of them! They are slightly fiery, but even friends who describe themselves as heat-intolerant have devoured these and raved about them. Jalapeños of any size will do, but the bigger ones hold more flavor and are easier to fill with cheese. And remember to wear disposable food-handling gloves when touching and coring fresh jalapeños, because the oil from hot chiles will stick to your hands. If you rub your eyes or other sensitive areas after working with the chiles, it can be painful. If the chiles are mild, however, gloves aren't necessary.

You can buy metal chile popper racks, but you can also use a cardboard egg carton. At 350°F (180°C), the carton won't burn and you can simply throw it away when you're done. Another big plus to using an egg carton is that the carton absorbs bacon fat. This means no grease flare-ups. You can enhance the hickory or maple wood smoke flavor in the bacon by using that type of wood for your fire, or you can add a little different flavor to your poppers by using apple, oak, or pecan.

8 ounces (225 g) cream cheese or Neufchâtel cheese, at room temperature

½ cup (58 g) shredded sharp cheddar cheese

12 large jalapeño chiles (green, red, or both), cored and seeded

1 empty cardboard egg carton, lid removed, or a metal jalapeño popper rack

12 pecan halves, toasted (see Note)

8 ounces (225 g) thin-sliced smoked bacon

½ cup (45 g) wood chips, soaked in water and drained, or 1 cup (90 g) dry wood chips for a gas grill

NOTE

You can toast pecans for more flavor before inserting them into the jalapeños. To toast, melt 1 teaspoon unsalted butter in a small cast-iron skillet over medium heat. Add the pecans and cook, stirring, until slightly browned.

1. To make the popper filling, combine the cheeses in a medium-size bowl and stir them together with a fork. Put the cheese mixture in a gallon-size zipper-top plastic bag and cut a small hole in one corner of the bag. Squeeze each jalapeño full of the cheese mixture. Place the cheese-filled jalapeños in the egg carton. Push a pecan half into each pepper. Wrap a half strip of bacon around each jalapeño and secure with a toothpick.

2. Fill your charcoal chimney with briquets, set the chimney on the bottom grill grate, and light, or prepare a fire in your smoker. For a gas grill, turn half the burners to high.

3. When the coals are ready, dump them into the bottom of your grill and spread them evenly across half. Scatter the drained wood chips on the hot coals, or put the dry wood chips in a metal container and place as close as possible to a burner on a gas grill. Place the jalapeños on the indirect-heat side of the grill. When the smoke starts to rise, close the lid.

4. Smoke the peppers at 350°F (180°C) for 1 hour and 15 minutes or until the bacon is cooked and the jalapeños have a smoky aroma.

2 tablespoons (30 ml) bacon grease or (30 ml) canola oil

1 medium-size sweet onion, chopped

2 red, orange, or green bell peppers, seeded and chopped

Five 15-ounce (425 g) cans pork and beans, rinsed and drained

One 15-ounce (425 g) can creamed corn

One 4-ounce (115 g) can diced green chiles

2 cups (450 g) chopped barbecued meat scraps (pork, beef, or a combo)

2 cups (500 g) sweet, tomato-based barbecue sauce

Beer or cola, if necessary

Wood chips

PITMASTER'S SECRET RECIPE BEANS

SERVES: 6

Smoke a casserole? You betcha. Savvy barbecuers freeze smoked meat scraps to use in dishes like this one. For casseroles such as baked beans that really only need to have their flavors blend, smoking low and slow is the way to go.

1. Add the bacon grease to a skillet and sauté the onions and peppers over medium heat until tender, about 5 minutes. Combine the beans, corn, chiles, meat, and onion-and-pepper mixture in a roasting pan. Stir in the barbecue sauce. Thin, if necessary, with beer or cola.

2. Fill your charcoal chimney with briquets, set the chimney on the bottom grill grate, and light, or prepare a fire in your smoker. For a gas grill, turn half the burners to medium.

3. When the coals are ready, dump them into the bottom of your grill and spread them evenly across half. Scatter the wood chips on the hot coals or place them in a metal container as close as possible to a burner on a gas grill. Place the roasting pan with the beans on the indirect-heat side. Close the lid.

4. Smoke at 225°F to 250°F (110°C to 120°C) for 2½ hours or until the casserole is bubbling and has a good, smoky aroma. You can also bake this indoors in the oven, covered, for 2 hours at 250°F (120°C or gas mark ½).

SMOKE-ROASTED RUSTIC ROOT VEGETABLES

SERVES: 4

If you can smoke bake a casserole, then you can also smoke roast. Smoke-roasted root vegetables take on smoke flavor at a higher temperature, generally around 350°F (180°C). If you like roasted vegetables in the oven, you'll love these. As an alternative method, you can also partially slow smoke vegetables, then transfer them indoors to your oven to finish roasting and crisping at a higher temperature. Substitute other root vegetables, such as parsnips, beets, turnips, and rutabagas, if you like. This recipe works well in a gas grill, too.

2 large carrots, cut into 2-inch (5 cm) chunks

2 medium-size unpeeled russet potatoes, cut into 2-inch (5 cm) chunks

2 medium-size unpeeled sweet potatoes, cut into 2-inch (5 cm) chunks

¼ cup (60 ml) extra-virgin olive oil, plus more for drizzling

Fine sea salt and freshly ground black pepper

2 tablespoons (2.5 g) chopped fresh flat-leaf parsley, for garnish

Wood chips

1. Toss the vegetables with the olive oil and season with salt and pepper to taste. Place the mixture on an 8 × 12-inch (20 × 30 cm) piece of heavy-duty aluminum foil or in a disposable aluminum pan.

2. Fill your charcoal chimney with briquets, set the chimney on the bottom grill grate, and light, or prepare a fire in your smoker. For a gas grill, turn half the burners to medium.

3. When the coals are ready, dump them into the bottom of your grill and spread them evenly across half. Scatter the wood chips on the hot coals or place them in a metal container as close as possible to a burner on a gas grill. Place the vegetables on the indirect-heat side. Close the lid.

4. Smoke at 350°F (180°C) for 45 to 60 minutes or until the potatoes are tender and the vegetables have a good, smoky aroma. Transfer the vegetables to a platter, drizzle with a little more olive oil if desired, and garnish with the chopped parsley.

INDEX